How to Use

MICROSOFT PUBLISHER 97 FOR WINDOWS

How to Use
MICROSOFT
PUBLISHER 97
FOR WINDOWS

KATHY IVENS

Ziff-Davis Press
An imprint of Macmillan Computer Publishing USA
Emeryville, California

Publisher	Stacy Hiquet
Acquisitions Editor	Lysa Lewallen
Development Editor	Margo Hill
Technical Reviewer	Trudi Reisner
Production Editor	Barbara Dahl
Cover Design	Regan Honda and Megan Gandt
Book Design	Dennis Gallagher/Visual Strategies, San Francisco
Page Layout	Janet Piercy
Indexer	Valerie Robbins

Ziff-Davis Press, ZD Press, the Ziff-Davis Press logo are trademarks or registered trademarks of, and are licensed to Macmillan Computer Publishing USA by Ziff-Davis Publishing Company, New York, New York.

Ziff-Davis Press imprint books are produced on a Macintosh computer system with the following applications: FrameMaker®, Microsoft® Word, QuarkXPress®, Adobe Illustrator®, Adobe Photoshop®, Adobe Streamline™, MacLink®*Plus*, Aldus® FreeHand™, Collage Plus™.

Ziff-Davis Press, an imprint of
Macmillan Computer Publishing USA
5903 Christie Avenue
Emeryville, CA 94608

ISBN 1-56276-502-7

Manufactured in the United States of America
10 9 8 7 6 5 4 3 2

This book is dedicated to Thomas E. Barich, mostly in gratitude for the fact that he didn't turn up as my tech editor for this book. But also because a whole lot of the work on this book was done using his electricity, his printer, and his space, and he remained reasonably civil when I brought down his network.

TABLE OF CONTENTS

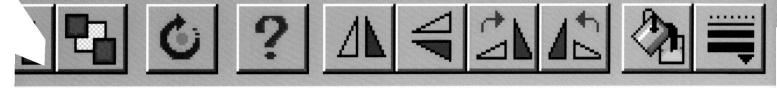

ACKNOWLEDGMENTS

The team that Ziff-Davis brought together to get this book into your hands was one of the most professional groups an author could ever hope to work with. Lysa Lewallen's support and help made this whole project take shape (and she's so much fun to talk to). Margo Hill, who kept the book (and the author) on track and on time, managed to do it with wonderful grace and good humor. Barbara Dahl brought everything together at the end. Carol Burbo coordinated zillions of details without letting anything slip through her fingers, an amazing feat considering I didn't always make it easy. And Trudi Reisner corrected my technical errors with such efficiency that I don't have to worry about being embarrassed.

INTRODUCTION

How to Use Microsoft Publisher 97 for Windows is an illustrated guide that takes you step by step through the features available in this desktop publishing software. These features are a powerful group of tools that make it possible to create professional-looking publications, and this book walks you through each step as you use them.

As you follow the steps, you'll see illustrations that match what you're looking at on your computer monitor. The steps are taken in their proper order, so you can follow them and end up with the same results. You'll learn how to make simple one-page documents, and you'll also learn how to turn out complicated publications.

You'll find that a great deal of attention has been paid to explaining the steps needed to put graphic elements into publications, because plain text is generally not terribly interesting. There's advice about making decisions, specific instructions to help you implement those decisions, and Tip Sheets to give you tips and tricks to enhance your knowledge of Publisher.

The later chapters explain some of the more complicated—and powerful—features of Publisher, including some publications that are just plain fun. There's also information about converting your publications so they can be put on the World Wide Web for all the world to see.

When you've finished this book, you'll be able to create a publication with confidence!

CHAPTER 1

Installing and Starting Microsoft Publisher 97

Now that you've decided to publish your own documents, you'll be amazed at how easy it is to get Microsoft Publisher 97 to produce them for you. Creating that first professional-looking publication is a snap.

In this chapter you'll learn how to install and start Microsoft Publisher, and you'll get a quick tour of the tools that are available to you when the software is up and running. The toolbar power in Publisher provides everything you need to point and click your way through the complicated parts of designing and executing a publication. (Of course, you'll have to provide the idea and the words that go with it.)

In the following chapters you'll learn how to design and produce the wide variety of publications that Microsoft Publisher offers.

How to Install Publisher

Installing Publisher onto your Windows 95 computer is very easy. Before you begin, close any software applications that are running. If you have a virus protection program that runs in the background, shut it down.

Insert the CD-ROM or Setup Disk 1 into the appropriate drive. In some cases, depending on your computer, inserting the CD-ROM automatically starts the Publisher Setup program. If that happens, you can move right to step 2.

TIP SHEET

▶ **Setup spends a few minutes looking through your computer to see if there are any copies of Publisher already installed. If it finds a previous copy, you'll be notified that the installation program will replace it and you'll be asked to confirm that it's okay to do so. Don't worry, your data files (the publications you've prepared) won't be deleted and will be available to you with this new version of Publisher.**

▶ **During the installation process you'll be asked if you want to install Postscript printing ability so you can send files to an outside printing service if you ever need to. To do this, you will have to find your original Windows disks to transfer the necessary files. Since you can do this at any time, it's usually better to say No to this query for now, even if you plan to use outside printing services for your publication.**

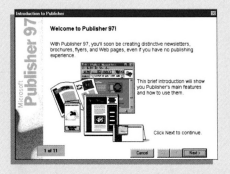

▶ **①** On the Start menu, point to Settings, then click Control Panel. When the Control Panel opens, double-click the Add/Remove Programs icon, then click the Install button.

⑤ When Publisher launches for the first time, the Welcome to Publisher 97 tour appears in the window. You can move through the pages of this mini-manual to get acquainted with the software's features. Just choose Cancel whenever you want to get back to the main window to start working. If you want to peruse it again, choose Introduction to Publisher from the Help menu.

As the Setup program begins its work, several screens are displayed. Just follow the simple instructions.

 Setup wants to know whether you want a Complete Installation or a Custom Installation. It's always safe to choose Complete because if you want to remove or add any features you can do that at any time. Just click on the appropriate icon to continue. Setup transfers all the necessary files to your hard drive.

 After the installation is complete you can start Publisher. Click the Start button and point to Programs. Then move your pointer to Microsoft Publisher and click on it.

Touring the Publisher Toolbar

On the left side of the main Publisher window is the Publisher toolbar. The people who use Publisher sometimes call it the Creation toolbar. In the documentation, Microsoft calls it the left toolbar. No matter what you call it, it's quick and handy. The collection of tools is a powerful assistant as you create pages for your publication.

Some of the tools operate as click-and-point, or click-and-drag. That means when you select them, you click on the tool and then point and click at the position on the page where you want to insert the tool's shape (that's click-and-point). You can also click on the tool, then point and drag your mouse on the page to determine the placement and size of the shape. The shape becomes a frame for the tool you selected.

Click the Pointer at the top of the toolbar to turn your mouse pointer back to its normal state after clicking a tool.

1 Click on the Text tool to create a frame that's ready to accept text. You can start typing right away, and if the type is too small to read you can press F9 to zoom in. If you know how to use the Format toolbar, increase the size of the font by using the Font Size button. (Information about the Format toolbar can be found later in this chapter.)

7 Use the Insert Object (OLE) tool to insert an object from another Windows software application. Use the Design Gallery tool to open a catalog of art work you can choose from to add zest to your publication.

6 Click the PageWizards tool and select a special page type to fill a page or part of a page.

TIP SHEET

▶ If you're experimenting with some of the tools and don't like the results, select the frame and press Del to make it go away, then try something else.

▶ WordArt, OLE objects, and the Design Gallery are powerful tools that can satisfy the most creative urges you have, and implement the most complicated projects you design. More information about using these tools is found in other chapters in this book.

2 Click the Picture tool to put a picture frame on your page. All you see is the frame until you place a picture in it. Right-click in the selected frame and choose a source for the picture.

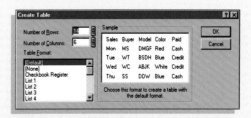

3 Click the Table tool and then click the page to see the Create Table dialog box. Specify the options to match the format you need. Click OK to put the table on the page, then fill in the figures.

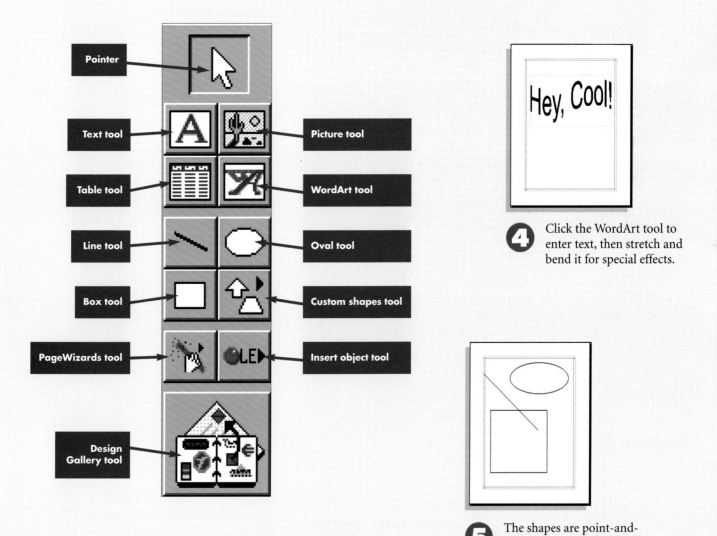

4 Click the WordArt tool to enter text, then stretch and bend it for special effects.

5 The shapes are point-and-click easy to put on a page.

Touring the Menu Bar

The menu bar in Publisher shares some items in common with the traditional Windows menu bars. You've seen many of those items before in the other software you use. But there are some menu items that are unique to Publisher, and some of the traditional menu items have commands that are special.

▶ **①** Many of the menu bar commands are specific to the type of frame you're working on and become accessible only if the selected frame can be manipulated with those commands. For example, look at the Edit menu commands when a shape frame is selected.

▶ When you use the File menu to Create New Publication or Open Existing Publication, any publication you're currently working on is closed. (If you haven't saved your latest changes, Publisher gives you a chance to do so.) Unlike most other Windows software, Publisher can only have one document open at a time.

▶ Many of the menu bar commands have shortcut keys (where you use the Ctrl key in addition to a keyboard character), shortcut buttons on a toolbar, or duplicates on a right-click menu. Using these substitutes is generally faster than using the menus.

⑥ The Insert menu doesn't change to match the object, but it offers lots of powerful commands.

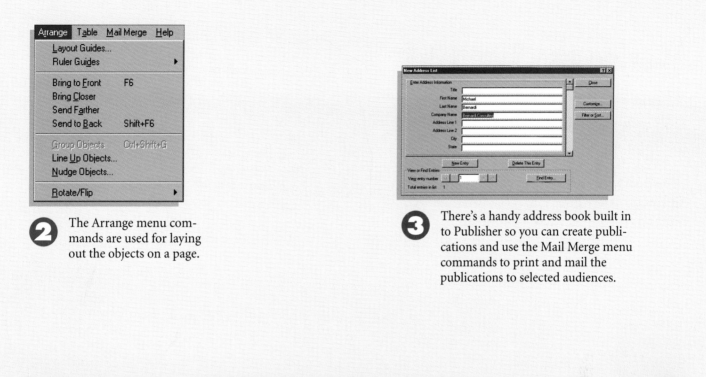

2 The Arrange menu commands are used for laying out the objects on a page.

3 There's a handy address book built in to Publisher so you can create publications and use the Mail Merge menu commands to print and mail the publications to selected audiences.

File   Edit   View   Insert   Format   Tools   Arrange   Table   Mail Merge   Help

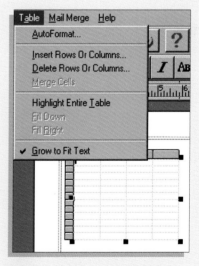

5 The Format menu is another chameleon—it changes its contents to meet the needs of the object type you're working on.

4 When you create a table, the Table menu helps you manipulate it.

Touring the Standard Toolbar, Status Line, and Status Bar

The working window in Publisher is framed on the top and bottom by a few elements that you'll use a lot as you work. The Standard toolbar is above the window, just below the Menu bar. The Status Line is the bottom-most element in the Publisher window (although it may not be the bottom-most element on your screen, because your Taskbar may occupy that space). Just above the Status Line is the Status Bar, which holds a couple of Publisher tools in addition to the horizontal scroll bar.

Most of these tools are duplicates of menu items and provide fast point-and-click access to Publisher features.

Like the menu command lists, these elements tend to adjust themselves to whatever you're currently doing. The Standard toolbar buttons are lit up and accessible, or grayed out and inaccessible, depending on your current task. The Status Bar displays information that changes as you move around your Publisher window.

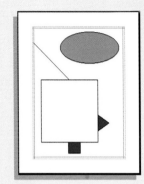

▶ **1** Clicking the Send to Back button moved the curved arrow shape behind the square shape. The Bring to Front button does the opposite.

5 On the Status Bar, click the plus sign to zoom in, the minus sign to zoom out, or click zoom number to see a menu of choices about the magnification.

TIP SHEET

▸ **To learn about features, keep an eye on the left side of the Status Line as you point to toolbar buttons and menu items. Every menu item and toolbar button is explained.**

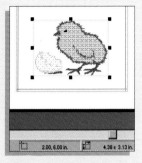

2 When a frame is selected, the Status Line shows the position of its upper-left corner in the Object Position box (the one on the left). The size of the selected frame is shown in the Object Size box (the one on the right). When no object is selected, the Object Position box shows the location of the mouse pointer (a pointer icon appears in the box) and you can watch the numbers change as you maneuver the mouse.

3 You can show and hide Publisher's Help Index and Help Pages with the Status Line buttons.

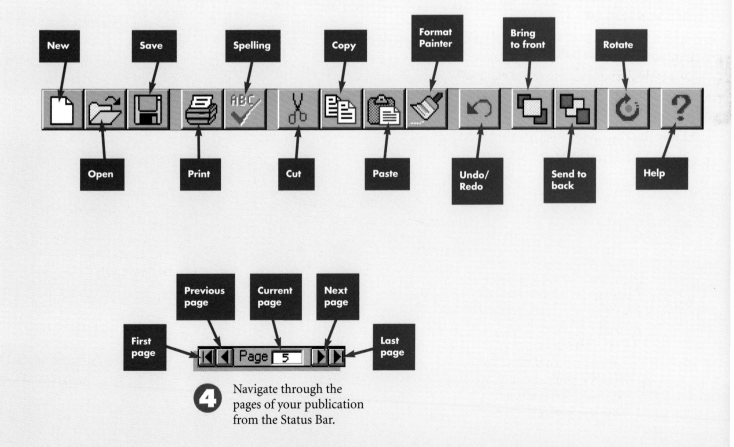

4 Navigate through the pages of your publication from the Status Bar.

Touring the Formatting Toolbars

Publisher provides specific formatting toolbars for different types of objects. They appear when they're needed and disappear in favor of other formatting toolbars when you change the type of selected element of your page. When nothing's selected, you won't see a formatting toolbar.

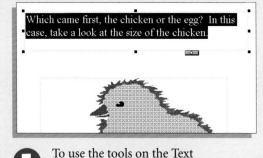

► **1** To use the tools on the Text Format toolbar on existing text, first you must select the text. If you want new text to have special formatting, click the appropriate tool, then start entering characters.

TIP SHEET

► Put together a group of formatting commands you think you'll use often and save the collection as a style by giving it a name. Then you can choose the style from the Style box on the Text Format Toolbar whenever the occasion demands.

► When you rotate graphics, the rotation is 90 degrees at a time.

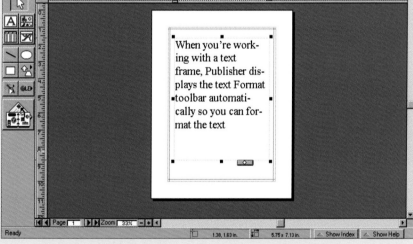

THIS IS A HEADLINE WITH SMALL CAPS

2 The Small Capitals button on the Text Format toolbar produces text that stands out.

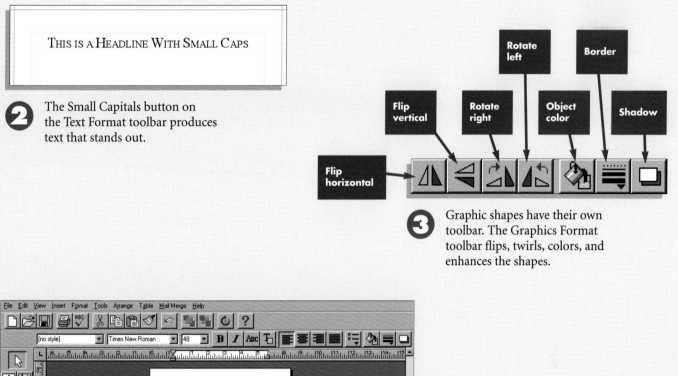

3 Graphic shapes have their own toolbar. The Graphics Format toolbar flips, twirls, colors, and enhances the shapes.

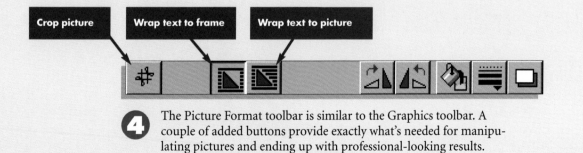

4 The Picture Format toolbar is similar to the Graphics toolbar. A couple of added buttons provide exactly what's needed for manipulating pictures and ending up with professional-looking results.

CHAPTER 2

Beginning a New Publication

Just to make working in Publisher a little more interesting, the software offers several methods for starting a new document. (Publisher uses the word "publication" as well as "document" to describe the work you do, and the terms are synonymous.) Each method has its own merits, and you can pick the one that makes you most comfortable. In fact, depending on the type of publication you create, you'll probably find you switch between the methods.

In this chapter you'll learn how to start a new publication, how to create a text frame, and how to add text to your text frame. You'll also learn about saving publications and opening them again later when you want to work on them. And you'll get a look at Publisher's Help system.

Creating a New Publication

When you first start Publisher, a publication dialog box appears to offer assistance as you create a new publication. Choosing a publication type from the Page Wizard begins a process of answering questions and making decisions.

1 To use the PageWizard, choose a publication type and then choose OK. For this example, a brochure is the publication of choice, so the Brochure PageWizard wants to know about your design preferences. Choose Next when you have made a selection.

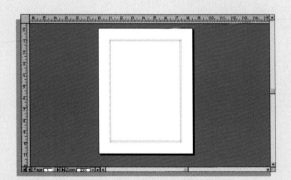

5 If you choose Cancel in the publication dialog box, the dialog box goes away and leaves behind a standard-sized blank page.

2 Keep moving through the PageWizard, making selections and answering questions. The choices vary depending upon the type of publication you're creating. Some publication types have only a couple of decision windows, others have a great many (and even they change depending upon your decisions in the previous window). Eventually the PageWizard tells you it's time to create the publication. Choose Create It!.

3 The design is ready for you to insert the text and graphics of your choice. The PageWizard even offers to walk you through those tasks a step at a time (you don't have to accept the offer).

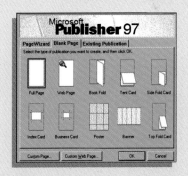

4 If you click the Blank Page tab in the publication dialog box, you have a choice of styles. Select one and choose OK to begin creating the publication. There aren't a lot of choices to make or questions to answer, but the basic layout of the publication style you choose is presented so that you can begin adding text and graphics.

How to Create a Text Frame

It would be very unusual to have a publication that didn't contain text (although it's possible to have one that doesn't involve graphics). No matter what you want to accomplish with your publication—selling an idea, explaining a concept, or announcing something—it's going to take words.

In order to place text onto a page, you have to start with a text frame.

1 If you've used the PageWizard, the design elements for your page (or pages) are preset. Text frames have already been added for you.

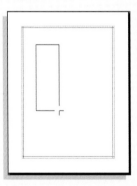

5 Another way to position and size the text frame is to click the Text tool and then place your pointer on the page where you want the upper-left corner of the frame to be. Hold down the left mouse button and drag the mouse down and to the right until you've created the frame size you need. Then release the mouse.

To add a text frame to a page, start by clicking on the Text tool.

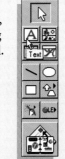

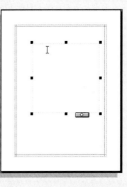

 After you've clicked on the Text tool, click on the page. A text frame is placed on the page.

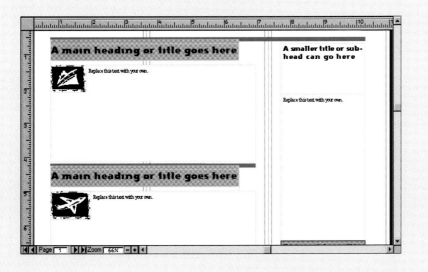

 To adjust the size of the frame, move your pointer to one of the handles on the edge of the frame. When the pointer changes to say "Resize," drag the handle inward to make the frame smaller, or outward to make it larger.

How to Add Text to a Text Frame

Once your text frame is in place, it's time to begin entering the words you need in order to make this publication do the work it's supposed to. When you start, don't worry too much about how the text wraps from line to line, or whether you'll need some text to stand out in some way. You can make those changes later.

 1 If you used the PageWizard to prepare your publication, click on any text frame to select it. When you do, the existing text is highlighted, so that as soon as you enter the first character, the place-holder text is deleted and replaced by whatever you type.

I'm typing like crazy but the text is so small it looks like I'm drawing tiny little worms. That's because I have this large frame on a large page and the font size isn't large. I can make the font size bigger or I can zoom in by using F9. Then I can zoom back out, using F9 again, to see what the text frame looks like in relation to the rest of my page.

5 Press F9 to zoom in on your text frame so you can see what you're typing.

TIP SHEET

▸ **The F9 key is a toggle: Use it to zoom in on a text frame, then use it again to zoom back out so you can see the text frame in relation to the rest of the page.**

▸ **If you enter text and it seems to disappear by rolling off the frame, don't worry. It's all there and later you can enlarge the frame or make the font size smaller.**

Begin typing your own characters where the place-holder text used to be. When you finish, click anywhere on the window outside of the page to take the text frame out of edit mode.

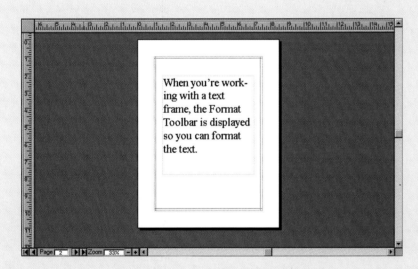

 To add text to a text frame you created yourself, select the frame by clicking on it. A blinking insertion point appears in the upper-left corner and you can begin entering characters. (When you first create the frame, it is automatically selected and the blinking insertion point is there, so you only have to take this step if you've left the frame and are now coming back to it.)

Many times, when you start entering text you can't make out the characters. They're just too small in relation to the size of the frame or the page.

How to Save and Retrieve Documents

Whether you've completed your publication or not, eventually you probably want to leave the computer and do something else, like eat or sleep. Or, perhaps something else needs to be accomplished on the computer, using a different software application. You have to save your document.

▶ **1** To save your publication, click the Save button on the Standard toolbar, press Ctrl+S, or choose File, Save from the menu bar.

▶ **If you're working on a publication and open another one, or exit Publisher, you're given a chance to save any changes in the current document. If the dialog box asking if you want to save changes appears, it means you have made changes that have not been saved (otherwise the dialog box wouldn't pop up). Unless you want to discard all the work since the last time you saved, choose Yes and save the document.**

▶ **When you are working on a publication and want to open another existing publication, the first one is closed because Publisher permits only one open document at a time.**

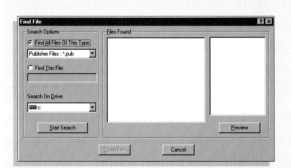

5 If you have saved Publisher files in different folders (perhaps you organize your work by type and use separate folders for different project types), choose Find File. Publisher will look for publications throughout your hard drive.

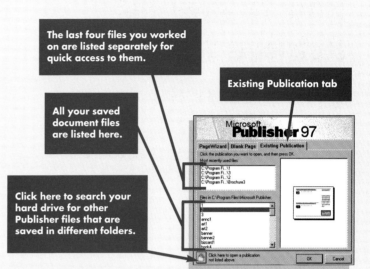

The last four files you worked on are listed separately for quick access to them.

Existing Publication tab

All your saved document files are listed here.

Click here to search your hard drive for other Publisher files that are saved in different folders.

2 The first time you save a publication, the Save As dialog box opens so you can give this document a name. Name the document whatever seems appropriate and choose Save. Publisher will add an extension of .PUB to the filename. After this, whenever you save this document it is saved under the same name.

3 When you first start Publisher, if you want to open a file you've saved so you can work on it again, click the Existing Publication tab in the publication dialog box. Select the file you want to work with and choose OK.

4 If you're already working in Publisher and want to open a document you previously saved, click the Open button on the Standard toolbar, or press Ctrl+O, or choose File, Open Existing Publication from the menu bar. The Open Publication dialog box appears. Select the file and choose Open (or double-click on the file).

How to Use Publisher's Help Features

Publisher offers help constantly. It's hard to do anything in this software program without finding some assistance being offered, even without having clicked the Help menu item. The automatic help messages are contextual, which means they contain information directly related to the task you're currently working on.

In addition, there is a robust Help system available from the menu bar, and a Help Index connected to Help topics right on the Status Line of the Publisher window.

▶ **①** When you work with the PageWizard, after the design of your publication is completed, it's time for you to add your text and graphics. For most publication types, when that step arrives, help is offered. As you move through the frames in your design, the appropriate Help contents window opens on the right side of the software window.

⑥ ToolTips provide explanations for every button on every toolbar.

2 The first time you perform a task, a Help pop-up window gives you some useful information. Publisher calls this feature "first-time help."

If you want to resize this object, position the mouse pointer over one of the square selection handles on the object's border, press the left mouse button, and drag the border. To move this object, drag the border between two selection handles.

Help
Microsoft Publisher Help Topics...
Last Help Topic   Shift+F1
Show Index   Ctrl+F1
Quick Demos...
Introduction to Publisher...
Keyboard Shortcuts
Help Text Size   ▶
Print Troubleshooter
Technical Support
Microsoft Office Compatible...
Microsoft Publisher Web Site
About Microsoft Publisher...

3 Click Help on the menu bar to see a comprehensive collection of Help features.

4 Quick Demos are like having a private tutor. Choose Help, Quick Demos from the menu bar, then choose a topic from the list that's presented and choose OK.

5 Click Show Index on the Status Line and pick a topic (just start typing and the Index will match your characters with words in the Index). Help on the topic you select is displayed in the Help window next to the Index.

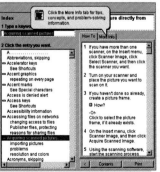

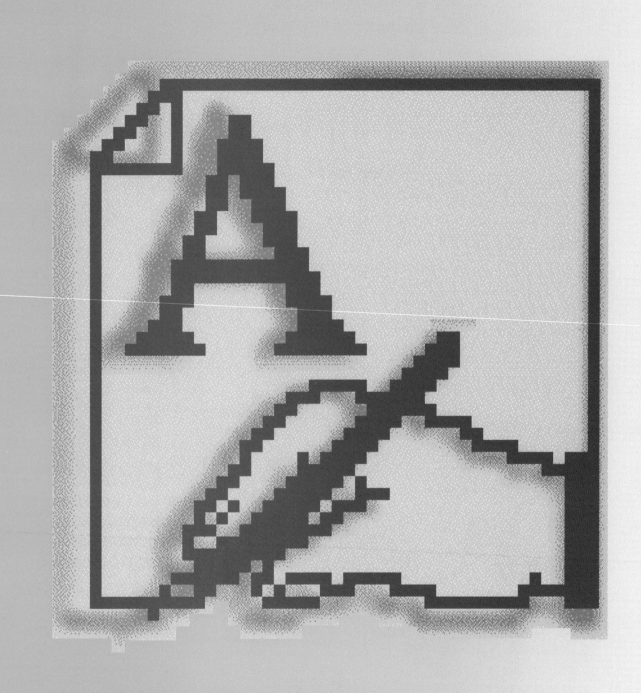

CHAPTER 3

Editing Text You've Added to a Text Frame

You've added text to a frame; it's brilliantly written. The words you've chosen will do exactly what you need them to do, the text is compelling, the message is perfect. Good for you!

You're not finished. You have to make sure all of that beautifully thought-out text gets noticed. Bold characters, underlined sentences, and special fonts (when appropriate) can make your words shine.

In this chapter you'll learn how to apply a variety of formatting features to your text, which will help you get your message across, and also make your publication look more professional.

How to Use the Font Formatting Buttons

Sometimes you have to emphasize words or phrases to make sure they're read or to make sure the readers understand how important they are. Other times italic type is expected, such as when you're referring to a magazine title or a foreign phrase.

The best way to produce a good publication is to worry about the words first, and the formatting second. Type in your text, then make the changes in appearance. Bold, italic, and other formatting changes can be accomplished easily from the Text Format toolbar.

1 To change the formatting of text, select the section of text you want to change. You can select as much text as you wish.

6 To put a border around the selected text frame, click the Border button and choose a line style from the choices that are displayed. You can see additional styles for border lines by clicking More.

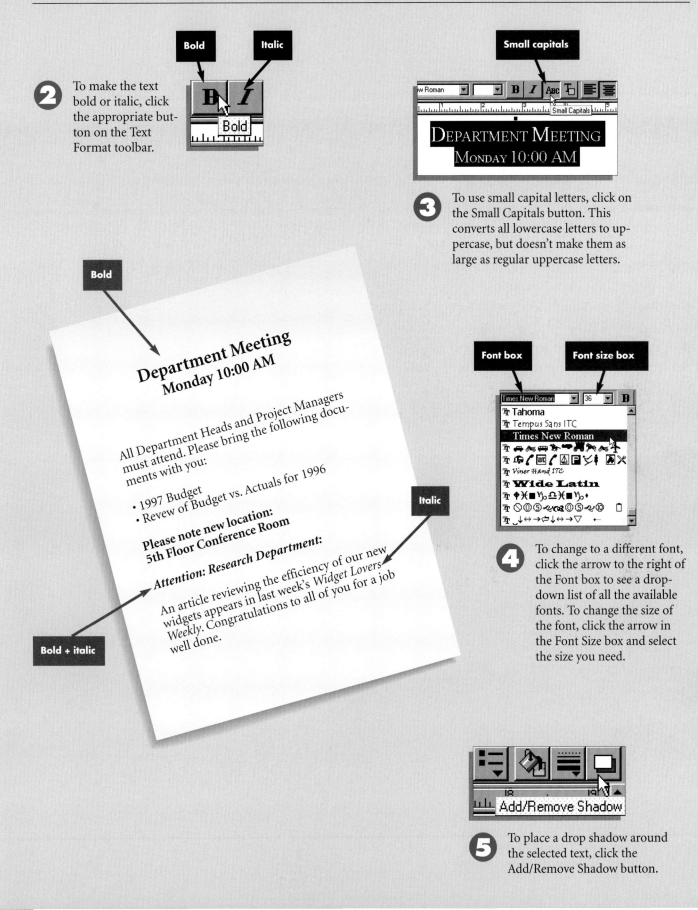

2 To make the text bold or italic, click the appropriate button on the Text Format toolbar.

3 To use small capital letters, click on the Small Capitals button. This converts all lowercase letters to uppercase, but doesn't make them as large as regular uppercase letters.

4 To change to a different font, click the arrow to the right of the Font box to see a drop-down list of all the available fonts. To change the size of the font, click the arrow in the Font Size box and select the size you need.

5 To place a drop shadow around the selected text, click the Add/Remove Shadow button.

How to Edit Text from the Format Menu

All the buttons on the Text Format toolbar are shortcuts to items that appear in the Format menu. The menu, however, offers a great many formatting options beyond those on the toolbar. In addition, you can fine-tune some of the special formatting effects using the dialog boxes available through the menu items.

If you've been using word processing software, you'll find two big differences in the Format menu in Publisher: There's no Font choice on the menu (use the Character Command instead); and the text formatting items don't even appear on the menu unless you've selected a text frame.

```
Format  Tools  Arrange  Table  Mail Merge
  Text Style...
  Character...
  Spacing Between Characters...
  Fancy First Letter...
  Indents And Lists...
  Line Spacing...
  Tabs...
  Border...
  Fill Color...
  Fill Patterns and Shading...
  Shadow                    Ctrl+D
  Text Frame Properties...
  Pick Up Formatting
  Apply Formatting
```

▶ **1** Select the text you want to create effects for and choose Format from the menu bar.

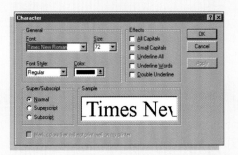

 Choose Format, Character for most of the common formatting tasks. The Character dialog box provides plenty of formatting choices, including fonts and effects.

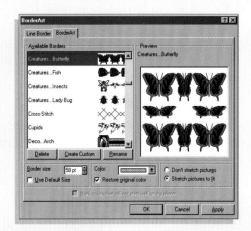

Choose Border to pick a border for your text frame. You can choose a line of varying thickness, and you can choose sides—your border doesn't have to appear on all four of them. Or, pick a fancy design that repeats itself all around the frame.

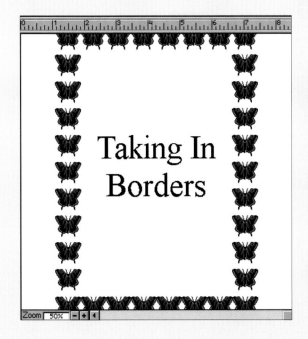

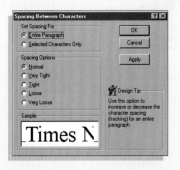

Choose Spacing Between Characters to tighten up your work—or maybe to loosen it up a bit.

 You can adjust your line spacing (Format, Line Spacing) to give your publication a professional look.

How to Save Your Text Formatting as a Style

As you use Publisher to prepare simple documents and more complicated publications, you'll develop some habits based on your own taste. For example, you may find you always use bold characters for headlines, italics for a subheadline immediately below the headline, and always center both of them. Or, when you do a newsletter, you may always format the headline with small capitals, bolded.

You can write down your formatting choices so you don't forget them, then you can create each type of publication from scratch every time you need to, or you can tell Publisher to memorize these choices so the style is available whenever you want it.

Creating a set of formatting options and saving them for future use is called *creating a style*. There are two ways to do this: format existing text and give it a style name (called creating a style by example); or create a style from scratch.

YO ! LISTEN UP

▶ **1** To create a style by example, format the text the way you want it to look every time you create this type of document, then select it.

TIP SHEET

▶ Styles are created for one set of standards, which means that you cannot create a style where there are two lines with two different formatting styles. If you select text that has two lines with different styles, the new style will take on the formatting of the first line.

▶ To change, rename, or delete a style, choose Format, Text Style, then select the style and choose the appropriate command.

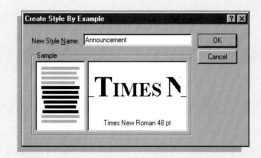

2 Click the Style box on the Text Format toolbar. As soon as you click on it, the style name is selected (the default style name is no style).

3 Enter the name for your new style and press Enter. The Create Style By Example dialog box appears with your style name displayed. Click OK.

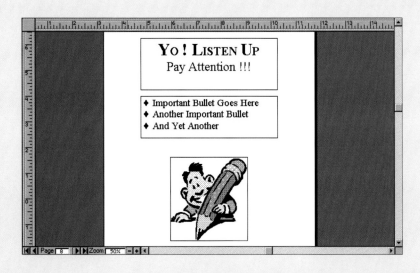

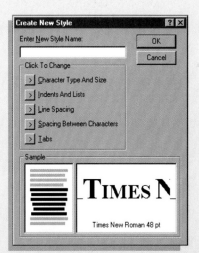

4 To create a text style from scratch, choose Format, Text Style to see the Text Styles dialog box. Select Create a New Style to bring up the Create New Style dialog box. Give the style a name, then choose the elements you want to customize. Click OK when you are finished.

5 To use your style, enter text and select it. Then choose the style from the drop-down list in the Style box.

CHAPTER 4

Changing How Your Document Looks on the Screen

 There are a lot of useful tools on your Publisher window. Some of them are used to create your publication; others are there to help you get an accurate view of what the finished product will look like.

Depending on what you're doing at the moment, there may be some tools you don't need. And it might be useful to clear some of the clutter from the screen by eliminating the tools you're not using. In fact, if you empty the window of elements, you have more room to work on your document.

How to Turn Off Toolbars, Rulers, and On-Screen Options

The tools available to you in the Publisher window are useful while you're working. When you're formatting text or inserting graphics, it's so easy to point and click. But if you're entering text and aren't ready to format it, and haven't yet begun working on graphics frames, you might want to clean off the screen.

Getting rid of Publisher's toolbar elements can actually result in more workspace, as you can see in the large figure on the right. You can enlarge your page and see more of it because it isn't cut off by those elements.

TIP SHEET

▸ **When you right-click to see the Toolbar listing, you can only toggle one element off or on at a time.**

▸ **If you want to bring back all the default elements quickly, choose Toolbars and Rulers from the right-click menu, which opens the Toolbars and Rulers dialog box. Choose Reset, then click OK.**

▸ **One way to get more working room on your Publisher window is to deselect Large Buttons on this dialog box. The smaller buttons that result take up less space.**

▸ **Remember that there's a trade-off for creating more working space by eliminating the tools—you have to go through the menu options to perform tasks.**

| ✔ Standard Toolbar |
| ✔ Format Toolbar |
| ✔ Rulers |
| ✔ Status Line |
| Toolbars and Rulers... |
| Help on the Workspace |

▶ **1** To toggle toolbars and rulers off and on, right-click below the Publisher toolbar on the left side of the window. The list of elements displays, and those with a check mark are currently on your Publisher window. Click on an element to reverse its current state.

5 If you want to set a ruler's zero point in a particular spot so you can measure the actual width or height of an element, place your pointer at the spot where you want the zero to fall. Then, with the mouse pointer a double-headed arrow, hold down the Shift key while you right-click. The zero point of the ruler moves to the spot you clicked and you can determine the size of the element.

Toolbars and Rulers

View
- ☑ Standard Toolbar
- ☑ Format Toolbar
- ☑ Rulers
- ☑ Status Line

OK
Cancel
Reset

☑ Color Buttons ☑ Large Buttons ☑ Show Tooltips

2 If you want to change more than one element, right-click and choose Toolbars and Rulers to see a dialog box that lets you select and deselect elements as you wish. Click OK when you have made your changes.

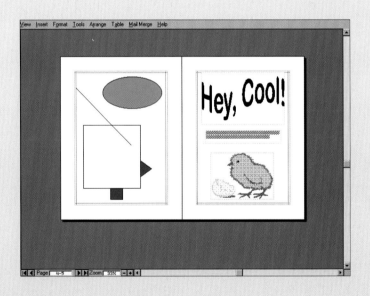

3 To hide the boundaries and guides for the frames and pages in your publication, choose View, Hide Boundaries and Guides. The individual elements in your publication are no longer displayed with boundary markers. To bring them back choose View, Show Boundaries and Guides.

4 If you want to move a ruler so you can see where a particular element will fall, position your mouse pointer on the ruler so you see a double-headed arrow. Then drag the ruler to the object you want to measure. Use the same method to drag the ruler back to its original position.

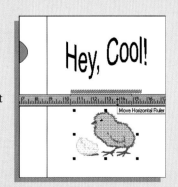

How to Insert Pages and Move between Pages

If you used the PageWizard to create your publication and told it you wanted a four-page newsletter or a three-page brochure, what happens if you haven't said everything you want to say when you've filled the publication? Don't worry, you can add a page. In fact, adding a page is so easy that sometimes it's just as easy to begin your project with a one-page publication type and then just add pages as you need them.

Once you've created a multiple page publication, there are some easy ways to move rapidly from one page to another, or to jump over a couple of pages to get where you want to go.

▶ **①** To add a page to your publication choose Insert, Page. This brings up the Insert Page dialog box. Choose the options you need and click OK.

TIP SHEET

▶ **To insert a new page quickly, press Ctrl+Shift+N. The new page is created after the current page.**

▶ **If you're creating a publication that is printed on both sides or is folded, you may have to add two pages to make everything work. If you can't think of more text to add, grab a piece of clip art to fill in (and amuse your audience).**

▶ **An efficient way to use the feature that duplicates objects on each page is to create a page with just the objects you want to duplicate. Then use the Insert Page dialog box to add pages with those objects (choose the Duplicate All Objects On Page Number option). Then go back to the original page and add the objects you don't want to duplicate.**

⑥ If you are working on the last page and need to add another page after it, just click the Next Page arrow (or the Last Page arrow). Publisher figures out what you're trying to do and asks you to confirm that you want to add another page. Click on OK.

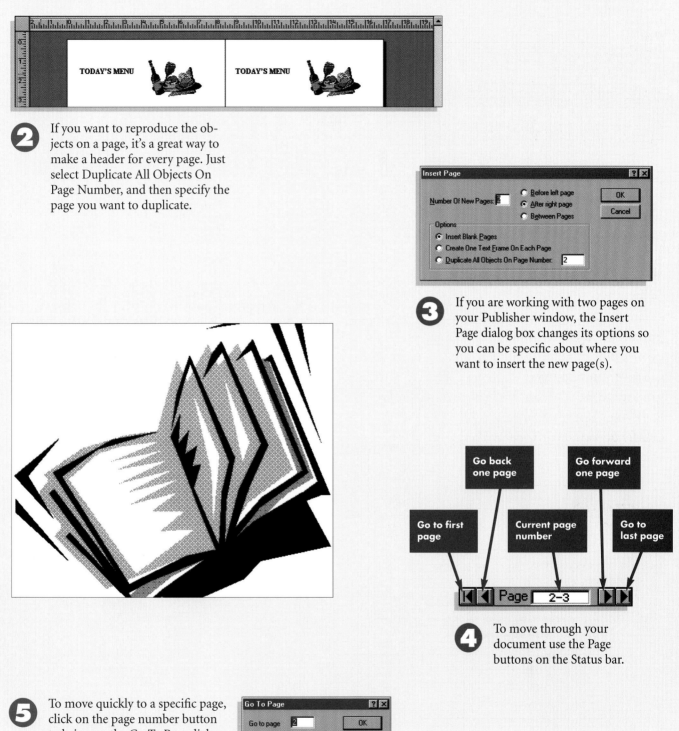

2 If you want to reproduce the objects on a page, it's a great way to make a header for every page. Just select Duplicate All Objects On Page Number, and then specify the page you want to duplicate.

3 If you are working with two pages on your Publisher window, the Insert Page dialog box changes its options so you can be specific about where you want to insert the new page(s).

4 To move through your document use the Page buttons on the Status bar.

5 To move quickly to a specific page, click on the page number button to bring up the Go To Page dialog box. The current page is selected so as soon as you type a new page number, the character(s) you type replace the information displayed in the page number box. Click OK. For even faster movement, press F5 to get to the same dialog box.

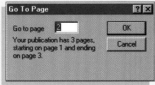

How to Use the Zoom, Scroll Buttons, and Viewing Tools

Publisher makes it easy to work up close by providing zoom capabilities. In fact, you can zoom in farther than you'll probably ever need to. Besides zooming in and out to get different perspectives on your page, there are a number of tools available to help you navigate through the pages of your publication.

The scroll bars and their buttons let you zip up and down, left and right, as you move to different parts of a page or a two-page view of your publication.

TIP SHEET

▸ **The Full Page zoom choice is the same as zooming to 100%. You won't see the whole page on your screen, but the rulers tell you where each element on the page starts and stops.**

▸ **When you zoom in, you're taken to the center of the page. However, if you have selected an object on the page, the zoom moves you in to the center of the object.**

▸ **To scroll quickly, click anywhere on the scroll bar. The scroll action will jump in large increments instead of scrolling slowly as it does when you click on the scroll arrow.**

Zoom 33% – +

1 You can use the Zoom tools to move closer or farther away from any object on the page. Click the minus (–) to zoom out and see more of the page. Click the plus (+) to zoom in and get closer to a frame.

Paragraph   Tab   Space

Attention: Research Department:¶
¶
¶
→ An·article·reviewing·the·efficiency·of·our·new·widgets·appears·in·last·week's·*Widget·Lovers·Weekly.*·Congratulations·to·everyone·involved·for·a·job·well·done.¶

5 Sometimes it's helpful to see characters that are involved with your layout but that never print. To see them on the screen as you work, choose View, Show Special Characters.

Click on the word Zoom or on the current zoom percentage number to pick a percentage for zooming in, choose to see the full page, or choose to see a page in actual size.

✓ Full Page
Actual Size

10%
25%
33%
50%
66%
75%
100%
150%
200%
400%

Zoom 33% − +

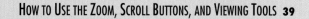

Use the scrollbar arrows to move the page across your working window (horizontal scroll bar) or up and down through the window (vertical scroll bar). To scroll more quickly, put the pointer on the scrollbar button, then click and drag in the appropriate direction.

To view two pages at a time, choose View, Two-Page Spread. The two-page view always shows the even-numbered page on the left and the odd-numbered page on the right. Therefore, you cannot see pages 3 and 4 at the same time. To return to single-page view, choose View, Single Page.

CHAPTER 5

How to Use Guides, Rulers, Margins, and Columns

Very subtly, working in the background, Publisher provides professional graphics tools for you to use as you design and complete a publication. Of primary importance are the layout guides. These are the pale pink and blue dotted lines that are displayed throughout the pages of your publication. They guide you through the structure of your publication, helping you fit elements properly onto each page.

There are several types of guides, including margin guides, layout guides, and ruler guides. Using them ensures that each page of your publication is consistent with the other pages. Headlines, columns, the bottom line of text on a page, and all the other elements in your publication will be consistent.

A good way to understand how all this works is to pick up a magazine. Notice that on many pages (or perhaps all the pages) there are stories and advertisements. You'll see that the columns for ads are in the same place on every page, and that the edges of the ads fall in the same place on every page. The bottom line for the editorial section of every page is in exactly the same place.

In this chapter, you'll learn how to use guides to keep your publications looking slick and professional.

How to Use Layout Guides

Layout guides are used to line up objects on a page. There are a number of ways to use this feature, but regardless of your approach, the object is to organize all the elements in a publication so the final product has a consistent, polished look.

Layout guides are consistent throughout the publication (as opposed to ruler guides, which are implemented on a page-by-page basis).

Layout guides are visible on the screen, but they don't print. The pink lines are margin guides, and the blue are layout guides (they usually fall in the same place for pages, and there are specific margin guides for text frames).

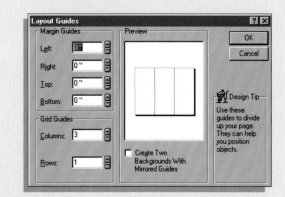

 1 You can view or change the layout guides by choosing Arrange, Layout Guides from the menu bar. When the Layout Guides dialog box opens, you can change the margins for the guides. By default, each margin guide is one inch from the edge of the paper, and you can change the setting for any margin.

5 The Snap To feature in Publisher turns the guides into a magnet that pulls the edge of frames onto the guide when you move the frame close to the guide. When you move a frame, as you inch along toward the guide the frame will snap to the guide itself. This is a terrific way to line things up without having to make nerve-wracking mouse movements that have to be just so. Turn on the feature with Tools, Snap To Guides.

TIP SHEET

▸ **If you want to see what your publication will really look like when it's printed, turn off the guides by choosing View, Hide Boundaries and Guides. Then you can view the document without all those pink and blue dotted lines.**

▸ **If you need to line up a page or column that has some objects arranged vertically and some side by side, select and align them separately.**

▸ **The Snap To feature is on by default for guides, rulers, and objects. You may want to turn some of them off, depending on what you're trying to align on your pages.**

Layout guides divide pages evenly. They actually sit on the background of the page and you have to manipulate them from the background. If you want to move the guides to create uneven divisions, with any page of the publication on the screen choose View, Go to Background (or press Ctrl+M). Put your pointer on the guide you want to move and press the Shift key. When the pointer displays the word Adjust, drag the guide in the appropriate direction. Remember that this changes every page in the publication. Use Ctrl+M again to return to the publication page.

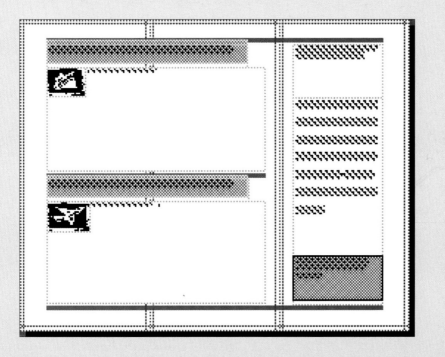

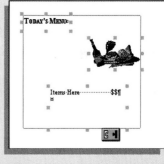

You can use the guides to align elements on a page. Select the element you want to align, or select multiple elements by holding down the Ctrl key while you click on each one.

Choose Arrange, Line Up Objects. Then choose the method for aligning the objects. The alignment is accomplished using the guides that surround the objects (which could be a column, a row, or a page).

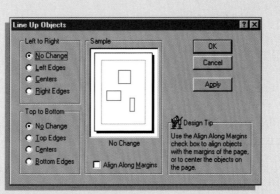

How to Use Ruler Guides

Ruler guides are lines you place on individual pages to set up the placement of elements on those pages. They're useful not only in aligning items correctly, but also in making it clear what the overall graphic plan is for that page (in case somebody else works on the page).

You can set vertical ruler guides to establish markings for the placement of the left or right edges of elements. Horizontal ruler guides help you place objects and text in such a way that either the top or bottom of each object is lined up at the same place on the page.

Set To Zero see P. 34

▶ **1** To create a ruler guide, place the pointer on either the horizontal or vertical ruler at the measurement point you want to set up as a guide. Press the Shift key, then press the left mouse button, which changes the pointer to a double-headed arrow with the word Adjust. Holding down the left mouse button, drag the mouse to the appropriate point on your page (use the markings on the other ruler as a guideline).

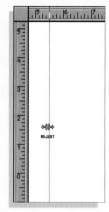

6 To remove a ruler guide, hold down the Shift key and then move the mouse pointer over the guide you want to get rid of. When the Adjust pointer appears, drag the guide off the window back to the ruler. Release the mouse.

TIP SHEET

▶ If you're adjusting frames to ruler guides, turn off the Snap To Guides and Snap To Objects options on the Tools menu. That way, as you get frames near your ruler guides, they'll snap to them instead of one of the other guides.

▶ To delete all the ruler guides on a page choose Arrange, Ruler Guides, Clear All Ruler Guides.

Once you've established the ruler guides you need (they are green lines), you can use them as you adjust existing frames or create new frames.

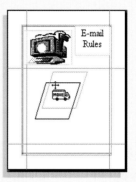

 To use the ruler guides, move a new or existing frame up against the guide you want to use as the alignment point.

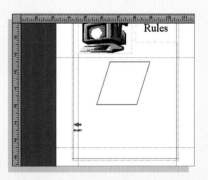

To fine-tune the placement of your ruler guides, press the Shift key and move the mouse pointer over the guide you want to move. Then drag the guide to its new position. However, any objects you already lined up with the guides will not come along, so you will have to move them to the guidelines again.

If Snap To Ruler Marks is enabled (checked) on the Tools menu as you create ruler guides, the guides will always land on a specific mark on the Publisher ruler (instead of landing somewhere between any of the eight measurement markings between each inch).

How to Create Indents

When you're working with text frames, there are times when you'll want to adjust the way text is placed so that it stands out on the page. A text frame is like a mini-publication, and frequently you'll need to divide the text frame in such a way that important information is presented differently.

One of the most effective ways to highlight printed information is to change the way it appears on the printed page. Indenting text on both sides creates white space around the text so it's easy to notice it. Indenting the first line of every paragraph gives a clear delination of each paragraph. There are plenty of ways to use indents to make your publication stronger.

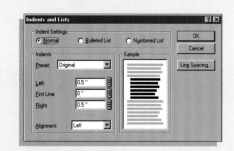

1 To indent text, highlight the text you want to indent and choose Format, Indents and Lists. The Indents and Lists dialog box displays so you can change the way the selected text appears. There are several preset schemes, or you can invent your own. You can see the preset schemes by clicking the arrow to the right of the Preset box. The list of preset schemes displays and you can select the one you want to use.

Marker for subsequent lines

Marker for first line of each paragraph

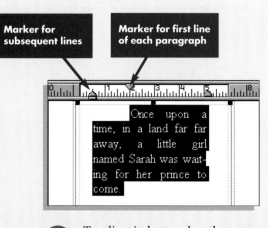

6 To adjust indents, select the text you want to adjust, then slide the indentation markers on the ruler to the appropriate place.

TIP SHEET

▶ When you design your own indentation scheme, don't forget to pay attention to the Alignment choice on the dialog box. You can align the text on the left, right, or center, or make it justified on both margins.

▶ You could use the markers on the horizontal ruler to set up indents without going to the menu system, but it is less exact than specifying measurements in the dialog box.

▶ To change an indentation back to "normal" text, select the text and choose Flush Left as the preset scheme.

2 Choose the preset scheme called 1st Line Indent (on the drop-down list under Original) to indent the first line of a paragraph and have all the remaining lines start at the left margin. You can use the pre-set indent value of .25", or specify a different number. Choose OK when you have made your selections.

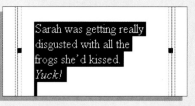

3 Choose Quotation from the drop-down list to indent all the selected text (it's as if you changed the left and right margins). The text moves in from the right to the same degree it moves it from the left. The preset indentation for both sides is .5", but you can specify whatever value you wish.

> Once upon a time, in a land far far away, a little girl named Sarah was waiting for her prince to come.
>
> Sarah was getting really disgusted with all the frogs she'd kissed. *Yuck!*
>
> She'd tried sleeping for a hundred years, but got wakeful and restless af-

> Once upon a time, in a land far far away, a little girl named Sarah was waiting for her prince to come.

4 Choose Hanging Indent to keep the first line at the left margin and have all the rest of the selected text indented. You can specify the size of the indentation.

Indents and Lists

Indent Settings
- ● Normal ○ Bulleted List ○ Numbered List

Indents
Preset: Custom

Left: 0.5"
First Line: 1.5"
Right: 0.8"

Alignment: Justified

Sample

[OK] [Cancel] [Line Spacing...]

 5 Choose Custom to design your own indentation scheme. As you enter numbers in the Left, First Line, and Right boxes, you can see the effect in the Sample box.

How to Create Margins and Columns

Sometimes the nature of the subject matter in your text frame demands special treatment. Either a page has to stand out when compared to other pages, or you need columnar typesetting to make your message effective. Sometimes it's effective to split a page into two text frames so you can change the margins in one, making it stand out on the page.

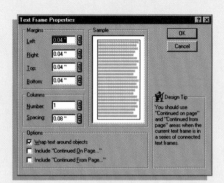

▶ **1** To create margins in a text frame, select the frame and click the right mouse button. Choose Text Frame Properties from the pop-up menu, which brings up that dialog box.

▶ For a small text frame, such as one that contains a headline, it's far easier to adjust the vertical placement of the text in the frame by changing the margins than by moving the text or changing the font size.

▶ If you're using columns, don't use a large font. It makes it harder to read and the wrapping is awkward.

▶ Did you know that television teleprompter copy is printed by creating one very narrow column? That's why you don't see eye movement while your favorite anchorperson is reading. The column never has more than three or four words on it (and they're all spelled phonetically). You can imitate this by creating a one column text frame with very large margins.

5 If the bottom of one column is the beginning of a topic (perhaps it's only one or two lines of the topic with the majority of its connected text in the next column) and you think the topic should start at the top of the next column, move the cursor to the beginning of the paragraph you want to move and press Ctrl+Enter.

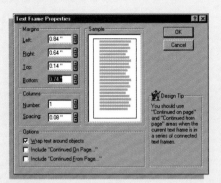

 2 Specify new settings for any (or all) of the margins. Keep an eye on the Sample section of the dialog box, which shows you the resulting effect.

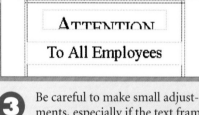

3 Be careful to make small adjustments, especially if the text frame isn't large. Large left or right margins can change the way the words wrap. Large top or bottom margins can roll the text out of the frame.

4 To set a text frame so that it becomes a columns frame, select the frame and right-click, then choose Text Frame Properties. When the dialog box appears, specify the number of columns you want in this frame, and also indicate the measurement of space between the columns (which is in effect a margin).

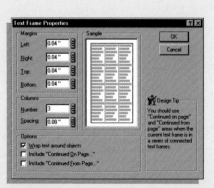

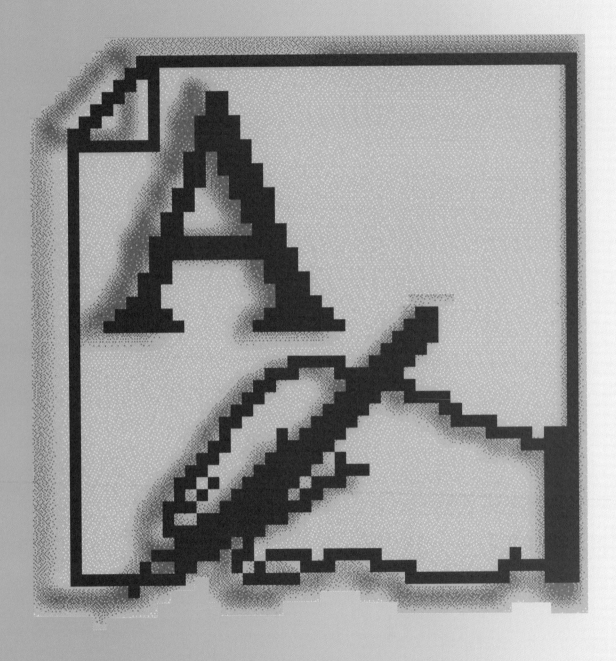

CHAPTER 6

Adding Clip Art to Your Publication and Wrapping Text around It

Part of the fun of creating a publication is adding art work to it. These graphics can be used to amuse the audience, make a point, draw attention to text, or give a visual description of what's coming next.

Clip art is art that is ready to paste into a publication. In fact, it gets its name from the fact that before computers, there were large sheets of paper sold with all sorts of graphic images on them. People who were preparing documents for printing clipped the individual art with scissors and pasted it on paper (along with the blocks of text). Then the printer took a picture of the paste-up and printed from the negative.

In this chapter, you'll learn about the clip art that's included with your Publisher software. You'll learn how to choose it, change it, and use text with it.

How to Select and Insert Clip Art

When you installed Publisher, you installed a large number of clip art files. In fact, the CD version of Publisher has more than 5,200 pieces of clip art. If you chose the Complete Installation option, only some of that clip art was transferred to your hard drive; you can always go back to the CD to use any clip art that wasn't transferred. If you used the Custom Installation option, you had the option of transferring all 68 million bytes of clip art to your hard drive.

If that's not enough to choose from, the Internet has many thousands of clip art files you can download and use.

▶ **1** To put clip art into a publication, you have to start with a picture frame. Click the picture tool on the Publisher toolbar, then create a frame on your page.

6 Most of the time, any word that you think might be a keyword will work. After you've typed the word, choose Find Now. It takes a few seconds, then clip art that is assigned to that keyword is displayed. For example, choosing the word *computer* produced all sorts of clip art related to computers.

2 Right click inside the picture frame and choose Insert Clip Art. (You could also choose Insert, Clip Art from the menu bar).

3 The Microsoft Clip Gallery opens with the Clip Art tab in the foreground.

4 The clip art gallery is divided into a number of categories. Scroll through the list to find the category you think will contain the clip art you're looking for.

5 If you're not sure which category has clip art with the theme you need, you can search for a keyword. Each clip art object is assigned one or more keywords. To search for clip art that fits certain keywords, choose Find in the dialog box to display the Find Clip dialog box.

How to Select and Insert Clip Art (Continued)

The Find command will look for any clip art files that are contained in the Clip Gallery. The files that are included with Publisher are a variety of art file types. In addition, you can import all sorts of graphic file types into the Gallery by using the Import Clips command and following the instructions.

7 If you don't think you can figure out the keyword, try entering part of the name of the object you're looking for in the File name containing box. You only need a partial name to search. For instance, if you need clip art that represents dancing or dancers, you can enter **danc**.

12 The graphic is inserted on the page.

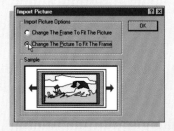

11 Since it's highly improbable that the art you selected is exactly the same proportions as the frame you created, Publisher wants to know what you want to do about that. You can have Publisher automatically change the frame to fit the picture, or change the picture to fit the frame. Choose OK after you've made a decision.

TIP SHEET

▸ Keep the Publisher CD in the CD-ROM drive when you're searching for clip art. All of the clip art is displayed in the Clip Gallery, but not all of it may have been transferred to your hard drive. When you choose clip art that is not on the hard drive, Publisher will look on the CD and fetch it for you. If the CD is not in its drive, you'll see an error message and you'll have to insert the CD or choose another piece of clip art.

8 If you want to search by name, it might be easier to browse through a list of file names instead of pictures. To see a file listing for the clip art and pictures, choose Insert Picture File (instead of Insert Clip Art) from the menu that appears when you right-click in the frame you've created for the picture. The Insert Picture File dialog box lists the Gallery contents by file name. Click on a file name that seems to match your needs to see the actual picture in the preview box.

9 The Clip Gallery also contains pictures. These are scanned images of photographs. You can insert a picture from the Clip Gallery by clicking the Pictures Tab. Then browse the categories and scroll through the pictures to find the one that suits your publication.

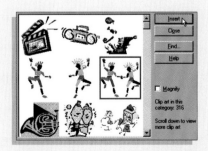

10 Once you've found the perfect piece of clip art, or a picture that conveys the thousand words you've been searching for, select it. A frame is placed around the object to indicate that it's been selected. Then choose Insert.

How to Resize and Reposition Clip Art

Once you've placed clip art on a page, you have to make sure its placement and size are correct. After all, it has to coexist with text, headlines, or even other clip art.

Getting everything "just so" is part of the fine-tuning process that makes the difference between a so-so publication and a slick one.

When you change the size of a clip art frame, the art it contains is resized at the same time.

▶ **1** Before you can manipulate a clip art frame, you must click on it to select it. To make the frame and the picture wider, move your pointer to either side handle. When the pointer changes to a Resize double-arrow, click and hold the left mouse button and drag in the appropriate direction. To make the frame taller, perform the same action on the top or bottom handle.

6 Sometimes the best way to make a frame smaller without making the clip art so small you can't see it is to crop the picture. That means you select a portion of the picture to keep and discard the rest. Click the Crop Picture button on the Format toolbar, then move the mouse pointer to one of the frame handles. The pointer changes to the Cropper (scissors). Drag the pointer and watch the grey line that indicates the cut-off point. Release the mouse to crop within the new line. If you want to crop another side of the picture, repeat the process with a different sizing handle. Click the Crop Picture button again to turn it off.

TIP SHEET

▶ To resize an object and keep its proportions the same, hold down the Shift key while you drag a corner frame handle. Be sure to release the mouse button before you release the Shift key.

▶ To crop a picture on both sides at once, follow the instructions for cropping, but hold down the Ctrl key as you drag the mouse. If you're dragging a side handle, the picture will be cropped equally on the other side. If you're dragging a diagonal handle, the picture will be cropped equally on all four sides.

Cropping
Resizing

2 To move two sides at once, move the pointer to a corner handle, and when it changes to a Resize double-arrow, click and drag in a diagonal direction. The two adjacent sides move equally.

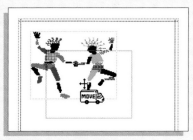

3 To reposition clip art, select it and move the pointer anywhere inside the clip art frame. This changes the pointer to a moving van. Click and drag the clip art to its new position on the page.

4 To keep the center of the clip art in the original location as you resize it, hold down the Ctrl key as you drag the sizing handle. Be sure to release the mouse button first, then release the Ctrl key. What this does is force an equal growth or reduction on the opposite side of the sizing handle you're using.

Scale Object

Scale Height: 256.10 %
Scale Width: 370.42 %
☐ Original Size

OK
Cancel

5 To change the size of a clip art frame with more precision, select the frame, then click the right mouse button to display the menu. Choose Scale Object to see the Scale Object dialog box. The numbers that appear reflect the current percentage of size compared to the clip art's original size. Increase or decrease the percentage as you wish. Type the same number in both boxes to resize the clip art proportionately.

How to Recolor Clip Art

If you have a color printer, you can take full advantage of it by recoloring clip art to get the maximum effect from it. Perhaps you have a defined color scheme for the entire publication (many annual reports adopt this approach) and want to change the clip art to be harmonious with that scheme.

If you're sending your publication to an outside printing firm, you might want to recolor the clip art so it can be seen on the screen, rather than write notes to the printer.

Even if you're printing in-house with a black and white printer, you can recolor the clip art to change the shadings and levels of grey.

▶ **1** To recolor clip art so that all the colors are the same shade (of the original color or a new color), select the clip art and right-click to see the menu. Choose Recolor Object to open the Recolor Object dialog box. Choose a color and click OK. This is a good idea for printing in black and white, or for using the clip art as background art (or "highly stylistic" art) if you are printing in color.

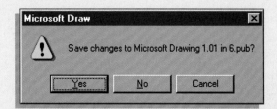

6 To go back to Publisher, choose File, Exit and Return from the Drawing menu bar. When you are asked if you want to save the changes in your original Publisher clip art frame, answer Yes or No, depending on whether you are pleased with what you did.

TIP SHEET

▶ **Recolorizing a picture so that it is shades of a single hue is an excellent method for colorizing pictures (scanned images as opposed to clip art). It makes the pictures much easier to reproduce on your printer, and provides an interesting result.**

▶ **If you're using a bitmapped image in your clip art frame, instead of choosing Microsoft Drawing from the Insert Object dialog box, choose Paintbrush Picture, which launches Microsoft Paint.**

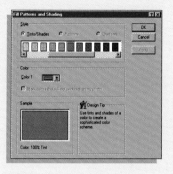

2 To use a fill pattern or shading, click the Patterns & Shading button and pick a pattern that matches your design plan.

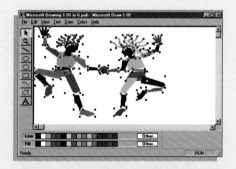

3 If you want to do a complete makeover of the colors in the clip art, you can edit it in Microsoft Drawing, a program that comes with Publisher. To start, you have to put the picture on the clipboard so you can paste it into the Drawing program. Right-click on the clip art and choose Copy Object.

4 Now you have to open Microsoft Drawing. With the clip art selected, choose Insert, Object from the menu bar. Then choose Microsoft Drawing 1.01 and click OK. When the Drawing program opens, choose Edit, Paste from MS Drawing's menu bar to place the clip art into the Drawing window.

5 Make changes by selecting the individual parts of the clip art and changing the color. You can add shapes and lines with the Drawing toolbar. If you need assistance, choose Help from the Drawing menu bar.

How to Wrap Text around Clip Art

Nothing screams "amateur publication" more than a page that has text in one place, a graphic in another place, and lots of white space between them. While this works fine if the graphic is a logo or some other design that should stand alone, most of the time graphics are used to enhance text and should be married (so to speak) to the text they enhance.

The way this works best, and most professionally, is to wrap text around a graphic. You can do this on a single column page by having the margin next to the graphic move to accommodate the graphic, or in a multiple column page to have the appropriate margins move to make room for a graphic between the columns.

1 Start with a text page, either a regular page full of text or a page of text in columns.

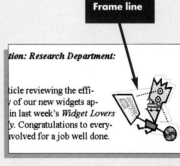

Frame line

5 If the text is a bit irregular when you change the method of wrapping text, you might want to move the graphic a bit. Notice that the frame line is now irregular instead of a rectangle.

Attention: Research Department:

An article reviewing the efficiency of our new widgets appears in last week's *Widget Lovers Weekly*. Congratulations to everyone involved for a job well done.

2 Click the Picture tool, then create a graphic frame by clicking on the appropriate part of the page and dragging the mouse to create the frame.

Attention: Research Department:

An article reviewing the efficiency of our new widgets appears in last week's *Widget Lovers Weekly*. Congratulations to everyone involved for a job well done.

3 Right-click in the graphic frame and select Insert Clip Art. Use the instructions at the beginning of this chapter to choose and insert the clip art you want to use. When the clip art is inserted, the text moves itself around the frame.

4 By default, the text is wrapped around the clip art frame, which is a regular shape. To wrap text around the shape of the clip art itself, right-click in the clip art frame and choose Object Frame Properties from the menu. Then select Picture Only, and choose OK.

TRY IT!

Now it's time to use the information you learned in the first six chapters. Follow the steps to create a publication of your own. In this exercise you will produce a sign you can put on the telephone poles in your neighborhood to advertise a garage sale. As you go through the steps, the chapter that covered the information is noted for you in case you want to go back to refresh your knowledge.

From the Start menu, put your pointer on Programs, then click on Microsoft Publisher. *Chapter 1.*

2

When the Publisher opening window appears, choose Cancel to begin working on your own blank page. *Chapter 2.*

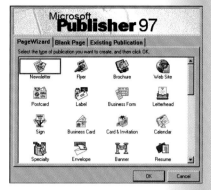

3

Go to the Publisher toolbar and click the Text tool so you can create a text frame. *Chapters 1 and 2.*

4

Put the pointer in the upper-left corner of your blank page. Hold down the left mouse button and drag down and to the right to create a text box at the top of the page. *Chapter 2.*

5

Press F9 to zoom in on your text frame so you can see what you're typing. Enter the text **Garage Sale**. Press Enter to move to the next line and type **Lots of Bargains**. *Chapter 2.*

6

Place your pointer at the beginning of the first line and hold down the left button while you drag your mouse across the characters to select this line of copy. *Chapter 3.*

7

Click the arrow next to the Font Size box on the Format toolbar and select a font and font size large enough to make this text a headline. In this case, choose Times New Roman, and choose 72 points. *Chapter 3.*

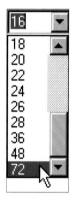

8

With the text still selected, click the Center button on the Format toolbar to move the text to the center of the frame. *Chapter 1.*

Continue to next page ▶

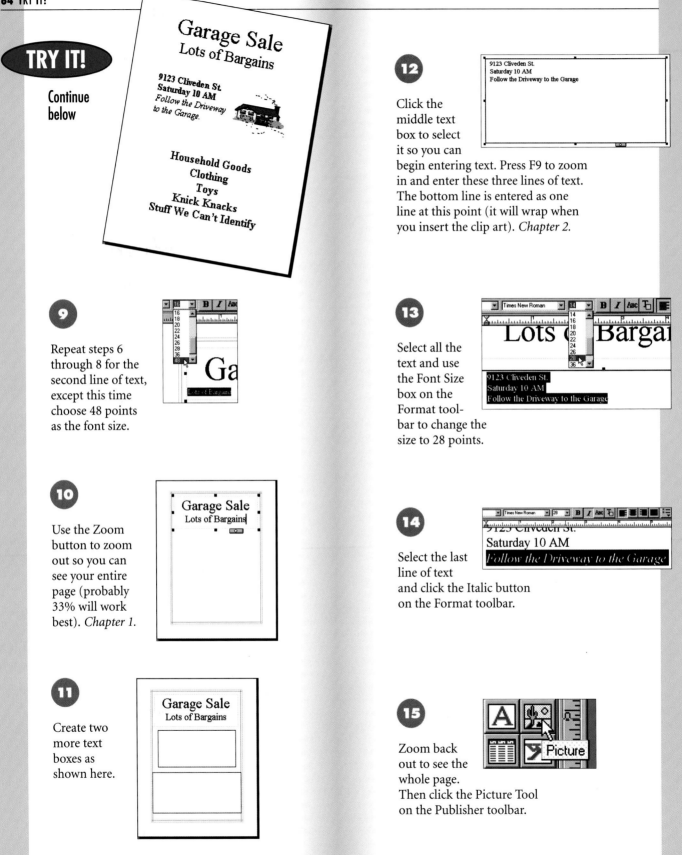

Continue below

Garage Sale
Lots of Bargains

9123 Cliveden St.
Saturday 10 AM
Follow the Driveway to the Garage.

Household Goods
Clothing
Toys
Knick Knacks
Stuff We Can't Identify

9

Repeat steps 6 through 8 for the second line of text, except this time choose 48 points as the font size.

10

Use the Zoom button to zoom out so you can see your entire page (probably 33% will work best). *Chapter 1.*

11

Create two more text boxes as shown here.

12

Click the middle text box to select it so you can begin entering text. Press F9 to zoom in and enter these three lines of text. The bottom line is entered as one line at this point (it will wrap when you insert the clip art). *Chapter 2.*

13

Select all the text and use the Font Size box on the Format toolbar to change the size to 28 points.

14

Select the last line of text and click the Italic button on the Format toolbar.

15

Zoom back out to see the whole page. Then click the Picture Tool on the Publisher toolbar.

16

Drag your mouse to insert a graphic frame on the right side of this text frame.

17

Right-click in this new graphic frame and select Insert Clip Art from the menu. *Chapter 6.*

18

Select the clip art you want to use and choose Insert (the clip art for this example is from the Places category). *Chapter 6.*

19

Choose to make the frame fit the picture and click on OK. *Chapter 6.*

20

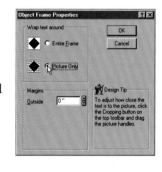

Use the sizing handles and/or moving van to adjust the size and position of your clip art. *Chapter 6.*

21

Right-click on the clip art frame and select Object Frame Properties. Then choose to wrap text around the Picture Only. *Chapter 6.*

22

Click the bottom text frame to select it and enter text as seen here. Then select the text, make it bold, centered, and 36 points. *Chapter 3.*

> **Household Goods**
> **Clothing**
> **Toys**
> **Knick Knacks**
> **Stuff We Can't Identify**

22

To see what your page really looks like, hide the boundaries and guides by choosing View, Hide Boundaries and Guides. *Chapter 4.*

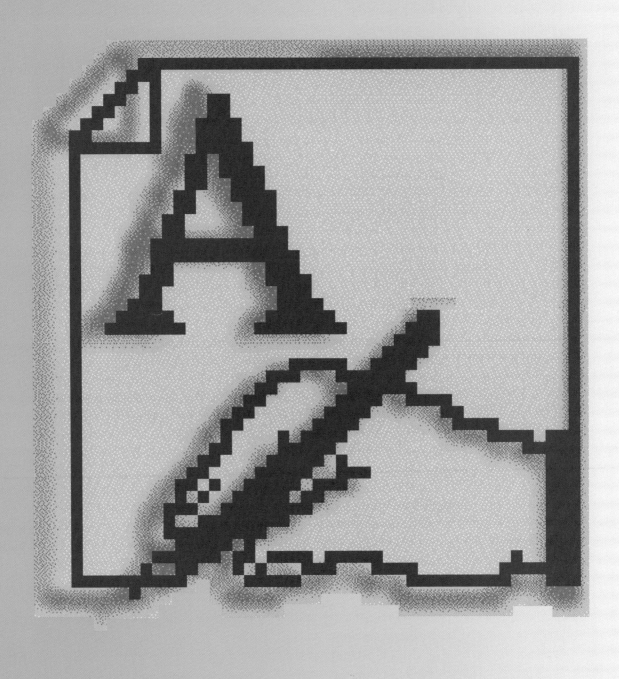

CHAPTER 7

Editing Text Frames

When you're writing a story or an article for your publication, it frequently turns out that it doesn't fit on one page. Even when you think you'll be able to get all your ideas onto the page, once you adjust the font size, bold some of the characters for emphasis, and indent some of the important lines, the text doesn't always fit. And if you add a graphic (which usually makes things more interesting and is so easy to do in Publisher) you lose a lot of space.

In this chapter you'll learn what to do with that text that didn't fit but that you don't want to cut out of your article. And, you'll also get some ideas for manipulating the frames that contain your text, dressing them up a bit.

How to Flow Text between Text Frames

Picture this: You're typing away and you get near the bottom of the text frame and suddenly you can't see the characters you're typing. You've overrun the text frame. But, unlike a word processor, a new page isn't created automatically so your text can continue. There aren't any error messages, there's no scroll bar to use to move down to where your characters seem to be landing, you can't see what you're typing. Where is all this text you're typing? It's hiding, and Publisher gives you some clues about what's going on.

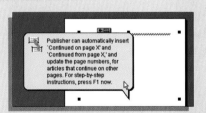

1 When you first create a text frame and begin entering characters, there's a button at the bottom of the frame. The button, which is called a connect button, displays messages about the size of the contents of the frame. It starts out by displaying a diamond. The diamond means that all the text is being held inside the text frame.

▶ **If your publication is already set up with multiple text pages, you don't have to create a new one, just move to any page with a text frame (or any existing blank page, and use the Text Tool to create a text frame). Then pour the pitcher into it.**

▶ **You can create a new page for the overflow text anywhere; it doesn't have to be the very next page. You might want to move past existing pages and create a new page at the end of the publication. Stories don't have to be on contiguous pages (that's why you'll learn about "continued on page x" in the next section).**

6 Before the pitcher empties, Publisher tells you that you might want to consider saying "Continued on page X" on the previous page and "Continued from page X" on this new page. You might want to do that, but not now. Don't worry, we'll cover that soon.

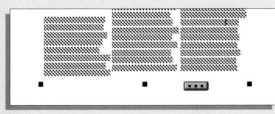

2 As you continue to type and you run out of room in the frame, Publisher stores the characters you can't see. And it announces that it's holding characters in an overflow area by changing the symbol on the connect button to three dots.

3 Now you have an overflowing text frame and Publisher has the overflow contents tucked away safely. You need to put this extra stuff into a new text frame. That requires two steps: First you must grab the overflow text in its own container, then you have to create a new text frame to accept your container full of text. Start by creating the container, which requires that you click on the connect button (which is displaying three dots). This turns your pointer into a pitcher, which holds the overflow.

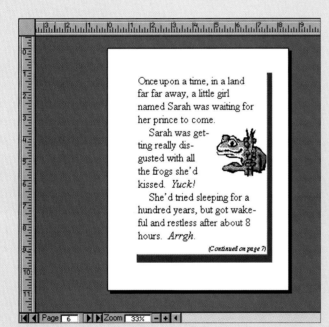

Once upon a time, in a land far far away, a little girl named Sarah was waiting for her prince to come.

Sarah was getting really disgusted with all the frogs she'd kissed. *Yuck!*

She'd tried sleeping for a hundred years, but got wakeful and restless after about 8 hours. *Arrgh.*

(Continued on page 7)

Insert Page

Number Of New Pages: 1

○ Before Current Page
● After Current Page

OK

Cancel

Options
○ Insert Blank Pages
● Create One Text Frame On Each Page
○ Duplicate All Objects On Page Number: 13

4 Now you need an empty text frame. The quickest way to do this is to insert a new page that's ready to accept the overflow text. Choose Insert, Page and when the Insert Page dialog box appears, specify a new page after the current page, and select Create One Text Frame On Each Page. Then choose OK.

5 When you move your pointer onto the new page, the pitcher has tilted, and you can see things spilling out of it. All you have to do is click on the page to put the text on the page. Click quickly before all your words fall on the floor.

How to Flow Text between Text Frames (Continued)

Now that you've poured your overflow text into a new text page, there are a couple of items to learn about. We'll look at the messages Publisher is giving you with the connect buttons and we'll work on providing a smooth segue for your readers by referring them to the proper pages in order to read your story.

▶ **7** Once the overflow text is placed in a new page, you can see if you're finished. Check the button at the bottom of the page. If there's a diamond symbol on it, all the overflow text fit on this page. If there are three dots on it, there's still more text in the pitcher and you have to create or find another blank page with a text frame and pour the overflow into it. Notice that the top of this page has a connect button with an arrow pointing left. If you click on the button, you'll go back to the previous page for this story. (The previous page has a similar connect button, but the arrow is pointing to the right. Click on it to move to the next page of the story.)

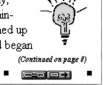

(Continued on page 8)

12 If you do eliminate a page in a connected series of pages, go to the blank page and disconnect it. To disconnect, click on the chain link symbol. In fact, you can disconnect a page that isn't blank (the text that was on the page is put into the overflow pitcher) and reconnect your story to a different page if you wish (just pour the text into the text frame of the new page).

TIP SHEET

▸ **If you accidentally delete the page number when you're editing the "Continued..." message, choose Insert, Page Numbers from the menu bar to replace the code.**

▸ **You can also change the font, the font size, and the attributes (bold, italic) for the "Continued..." notice.**

Text Frame Properties

Margins
Left: 0.04 "
Right: 0.04 "
Top: 0.04 "
Bottom: 0.04 "

Columns
Number: 1
Spacing: 0.08 "

Sample

OK
Cancel

Design Tip
You should use "Continued on page" and "Continued from page" areas when the current text frame is in a series of connected text frames.

Options
☑ Wrap text around objects
☑ Include "Continued On Page..."
☑ Include "Continued From Page..."

8 When a story or an article spans multiple pages, you'll want to add a notice so your readers can find the next page of your story (or find the beginning of the story if they open to a page that's a continuation). Publisher makes this task extremely easy. Just pick any connected page for your story and right-click. Choose Text Frame Properties. When the Text Frame Properties dialog box opens, check the two Continued options at the bottom. Repeat this step for each page in the connection chain.

Once upon a time, in a land far far away, a little girl named Sarah was waiting for her prince to come.

Sarah was getting really disgusted with all the frogs she'd kissed. *Yuck!*

She'd tried sleeping for a hundred years, but got wakeful and restless after about 8 hours. *Arrgh.*

(Continued on page 7)

(Continued from page 6)

Somebody told her about putting a pea under her mattress, but a little investigation proved that had nothing to do with meeting handsome princes, it just caused back-aches (or mashed peas if you didn't have a light and delicate back).

Then, one day, Sarah had a brainstorm. She signed up with an ISP and began

(Continued on page 8)

Once upon a time, in a land far far away, a little girl named Sarah was waiting for her prince to come.

Sarah was getting really disgusted with all the frogs she'd kissed. *Yuck!*

She'd tried sleeping for a hundred years, but got wakeful and restless after about 8 hours. *Arrgh.*

(Continued on page 7)

(Continued from page 6)

Somebody told her about putting a pea under her mattress, but a little investigation proved that had nothing to do with meeting handsome princes, it just caused back-aches (or mashed peas if you didn't have a light and delicate back).

Then, one day, Sarah had a brainstorm. She signed up with an ISP and began

(Continued on page 8)

9 The pages in your story have the appropriate messages about the continuation scheme for your readers. (Incidentally, the "Continued…" messages are really in small italic type—they've been enlarged in this illustration so you could see them.) If you insert pages in your publication, if you move pages around, the message will make the necessary adjustments to keep everything accurate.

hundred years, but got wakeful and restless after about 8 hours. *Arrgh.*

(Please Go To Page 7)

10 You can change the wording of the "Continued…" messages if you wish. Select the text you want to change and insert your new phrase. Notice that on the Text Format toolbar there's a Style Name for this feature. After you make the change, click the name of the style (there's one for Continued On and another one for Continued From) and press Enter. Publisher displays a message asking if you want to change this style to reflect your changes. Click on OK to do so (click on Cancel if you change your mind). Hereafter your new phrase will be used for that continuation message. Repeat the process for the other (Continued From) message. Be careful not to delete or replace the page number—it isn't really a number, it's a code and it changes as page numbers change.

(Continued from page 15)

11 If the last page of your story is extremely short, you may have a layout problem. For a newsletter, this is no big deal, you just start the next story under the end of this one. But for brochures or other publications, this can leave an awful lot of blank space. Go back to the previous page(s) and see what you can do to eliminate this last page. Make the text frame larger, make the font smaller, make graphics smaller, or even cut some text out of the story.

How to Reposition and Resize Text Frames

There are a variety of reasons that might make it necessary, or at least desireable, to move (reposition) or resize a text frame. Perhaps you need to put a graphic above or below the text frame, or put a headline above columnar text. Maybe placing text in the center of a page with plenty of white space above and below it is effective for a particular page.

▶ **1** To reposition a text frame, select it so you can see the handles. Then place your pointer on the edge of the frame between any two handles. This changes the pointer to a moving van. Press and hold down the left mouse button while you drag the frame to another place on the page.

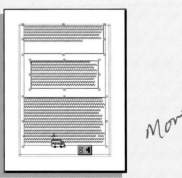

5 To move more than one text frame at a time, select each frame while holding down the Ctrl key. When you move your pointer to an area between handles on any of the frames, it will turn into a moving van. It doesn't matter which frame your mouse pointer is in, just begin dragging and all the frames come along for the trip.

TIP SHEET

▶ When you're repositioning a text frame, you can see two faint grey outlines: the original placement line and the new line (which keeps moving as you continue to drag). This gives you the opportunity to keep one side lined up if necessary.

▶ If you accidently move instead of resize (or the other way around), click the Undo button.

2 To resize a text frame, select it so that you can see the handles. To change the size of the text frame from one side, place your pointer on the handle for that side. When the pointer turns to a Resize button, hold down the mouse button while you drag in the appropriate direction.

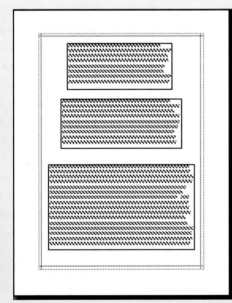

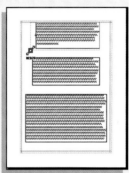

3 To expand or compress the frame on two adjacent sides at once, use the corner handle. The two sides adjacent to the handle move together.

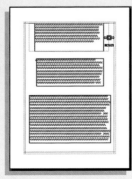

Resize
Ctrl-Key
Δ 2 sides at once

4 To expand or shrink one side and have the opposite side move the same distance automatically, hold down the Ctrl key while you drag the handle.

How to Recolor and Add a Drop Shadow to Text Frames

If you have the ability to print in color, either in-house or because you're using an outside printer, you should take advantage of it. One classic (and classy) way to use color is to put a color border around a text frame. You can make the border elegantly thin, boldly thick, or amusingly decorative.

Another way to add graphical interest to a text frame is to put a drop shadow around it. A drop shadow is an effect that is applied to two adjacent sides of a frame. The best way to picture it is to imagine the sun is on one side of your frame, so on the opposite side your frame is casting a shadow. If you want to put a drop shadow around a text frame, you can have Publisher do it for you or you can do it yourself. The latter is more complicated, but the results are dramatically different. When Publisher creates a drop shadow, it's quite thin (in fact I sometimes have trouble seeing it). And your only color choice is grey. Do it yourself to control thickness and color.

TIP SHEET

▸ If you added a color border and you also added a drop shadow, make sure they're color coordinated. The shadow should be a deeper shade of the border color (shadows are dark). Technically, shadows should be grey, but there's nothing wrong with having a more colorful approach.

▸ To enliven the text box even more, bring the shadow's box to the front and choose Format, Fill Patterns and Shading from the menu bar. Then pick a pattern for the color border. This is especially interesting if you are printing in black and white and did have to choose a grey border.

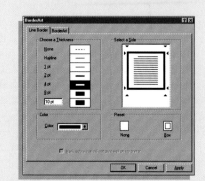

1 To create a color border, select the text frame you want to decorate and click the Border button on the Formatting toolbar. When the Border menu appears, choose More to display the Border Art dialog box. Select a border in the Choose a Thickness section of the dialog box by clicking on it.

6 Use the Send To Back button on the Standard toolbar to put the colorful box behind the text box. If the shadow is too deep, not deep enough, the wrong color, or there are any other changes you want to make (you might want to imagine the sun is on the other side of the text box which means the shadow will have to move), use the Bring to Front button to make the changes. Then repeat the steps to make it a shadow.

2 Click the arrow to the right of the Color box to see a color palette and click on the color you want. If you can't find the perfect hue, choose More Colors to see a wider selection. When you have selected the color, choose OK.

3 To create a drop shadow around a text frame, you start by drawing a box on top of the frame. Click the Box tool on the Publisher toolbar. Then place your mouse in the upper-left corner of the text frame and drag the mouse down and to the right to duplicate the size of the frame. I find it easier to work with the box that will become the shadow by making it just a tiny bit wider on the right than the text frame.

4 When you release the mouse, you see only the new box you've created. That's because the box is in front of the text frame. (You can switch their positions, just to reassure yourself that you haven't obliterated the text frame, by clicking the Send To Back button on the Standard toolbar, then clicking the Bring to Front button to put things back so you can work). Resize the new box to make its bottom edge slightly larger than the text box. If you didn't make the box wider on the right when you first created it, do that now. The bottom and right edges of the box have to show (and are all that will show) when this box becomes the drop shadow.

> Once upon a time, in a land far far away, a little girl named Sarah was waiting for her prince to come.
>
> Sarah was getting really disgusted with all the frogs she'd kissed. *Yuck!*
>
> She'd tried sleeping for a hundred years, but got wakeful and restless after about 8 hours. *Arrgh.*
>
> *(Please Go To Page 7)*

5 Now you can choose a color for the drop shadow. What you have to do is fill this box with a color (remember only two edges will show when you put it behind the text box). Choose Format, Fill Color to see the Colors dialog box. Click on the color you want to use for the border. Choose OK.

CHAPTER 8

How to Use Publisher's Advanced Text Formatting Tools

Once your basic publication is entered (your text frames are filled with marvelous prose, your headlines are compelling and impossible to ignore, the graphics you chose add just the right touch), it's time to get serious. Desktop publishing can look just as professional as the print jobs that come out of the offices on Madison Avenue.

In this chapter you'll learn about some of the text tools you can use to help make your publication a bit slicker.

How to Pick Up and Apply Formatting

When you finally get a page (or a text frame on a page) perfect, the first thing to do is save the document. What's the next thing you do? You re-create your perfection on another page. Sigh. All that work. Reinventing the wheel is a tiresome task.

Cheer up! Publisher figured you'd eventually get around to creating exactly what you wanted and they invented some tools to help you achieve the same excellence time after time without doing all that work again. The power of Pick Up Formatting, followed by Apply Formatting, is only a couple of mouse-clicks away.

▶ **1** To take the formatting of your text frame to other pages, begin by selecting the frame. Right-click to see the menu choices, and choose Pick Up Formatting.

TIP SHEET

▶ A mini-formatting copier, called the Format Painter, is available on the toolbar (its icon looks like a paintbrush). It works by selecting a text frame you want to use as a model, then clicking the paintbrush, then clicking the target frame to "paint" it with the same formatting. The pointer turns into a paintbrush during this process. However, I've found this only works with very simple formatting. If you have both bold and italic text in your original formatting, many times only the bold is transferred (the italic must get caught between the brush hairs).

▶ If you're creating a large publication, such as a newsletter, a multipage brochure, or a handbook, try my trick for formatting consistency. I plan (in my mind and sometimes on paper) what I want it to look like. Then I create one of each type of object frame (text, graphic, and so on) on the first page or two. I use them as templates to create lots of frames on lots of pages, transferring the appropriate formatting. After I'm finished, I delete those first pages.

6 If the source object (the one you want to copy the formatting from) and the target object (the one you want to copy the formatting to) are on the same page, use the right mouse button to drag the former over the latter (the jargon for that is "a right-drag"). When you release the mouse button, a menu appears. Choose Apply Formatting Here.

 Move to another text frame. If the page you're moving to does not have a text frame on it, create one. Right-click on the text frame and choose Apply Formatting.

Hey, nifty!

All the formatting is the same, even though the words are different. This means I can format my text page and no matter how much text I have to put into my publication, every page will look the same.

And, I won't have to click any menu options, or choose any formatting features to make that happen.

3 As you enter text in this frame, the formatting will match the page you used as the prototype. You can continue to right-click and choose Apply Formatting to additional text frames. In fact, during this session of Publisher, that formatting is in the Apply Formatting memory whenever you choose to use it. If you choose another object and select Pick Up Formatting, the new formatting scheme is placed into the Apply Formatting memory.

HEADLINE WITH SMALL CAPS
And a Subheadline That's Italic

Body Text goes here.

All Text is 24 pt Times New Roman and is Bold. The page is left justified. The spacing between lines has been increased to 1.25 spaces instead of the default 1 space. There is an extra 4 point space after each paragraph

4 You can perform the same duplication of formatting for other objects, such as graphics, where you can opt to wrap text around the graphic frame or the graphic picture itself. Insert your graphic and then tweak the formatting so everything is exactly the way you want it. Then choose Pick Up Formatting from the right-click menu.

 Move to another page (with the same object type) and choose Apply Formatting from the right-click menu. In this example, the object was clip art, and the formatting (text wraps around the object, not the frame, and there is a margin around the object) is the same for the coffee cup as for the chicken and egg. In fact, by continuing to choose Apply Formatting in every clip art frame in the publication, the consistency of this publication is assured.

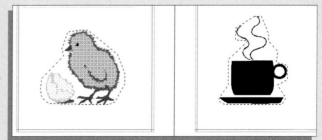

Character and Line Spacing

What if your text just doesn't fit properly in the frame—it almost makes it, but not quite? Sometimes a couple of lines have to flow into another frame and you have nothing more to say so that second frame looks rather naked. Sometimes your story ends and there's a big chunk of empty white space at the bottom of the page.

One nifty way to fix this is to adjust the way characters and lines are spaced. Push everything together just a bit more and you can probably get rid of that small amount of overflow text. Separate everything a little and you can fill a page.

1 You can change the spacing between lines for the paragraph in which your pointer sits, or for a specific block of text (you have to select the block of text first). Choose Format, Line Spacing from the menu bar.

E-Mail Rules

7 In this example, the resulting display works quite well.

6 To do this, select E-M from the headline and open the Spacing Between Characters dialog box. Choose Selected Characters Only. Then choose whether you want to Squeeze Letters Together or Move Letters Apart. In the By This Amount box, use the arrows to specify the amount by which you are squeezing (or separating). Keep an eye on the Sample box at the bottom of the dialog box.

TIP SHEET

▶ You can create a serious readability problem if you change the line spacing too much. It can give readers eyestrain or a headache to try to follow text that has the top of the characters on one line meeting the bottom of the characters on the line above.

▶ It's not a good idea to tighten up character spacing with fonts that have a lot of fancy edges on the characters—they'll bump into each other and the text will be difficult to read.

2 You can change the spacing options between Lines at intervals of one-fourth of a space at a time. The size (height) of the space matches the size of the font. You can also change the spacing Before and After Paragraphs in measurements of points. This illustration shows the difference between line spacing of three-quarters of a space (the top paragraph) and a full space (the bottom paragraph).

| This paragraph is set for normal line spacing | This paragraph has spacing that is set for 1.25 lines of space. | This paragraph has spacing that is set for 75% of the normal line spacing. |
| The characters in this paragraph are set for normal spacing | The characters in this paragraph are set for tight spacing | The characters in this paragraph are set for loose spacing |

E-Mail Rules

5 Selecting specific characters in order to adjust the spacing between them is usually helpful for headlines. This headline would look a bit more professional if the letters in the hyphenated word E-Mail were a bit closer together.

3 Changing the spacing between paragraphs means you don't have to press Enter twice to create a blank line. You can press Enter once and let the formatting option insert space before the next paragraph. In this illustration the Enter key was pressed once between the first and second paragraphs and the line spacing before paragraphs was set for half as many points as the size of the font. You can see that it's quite easy to see the delineation between paragraphs. The space between the second and third paragraphs was not altered in the dialog box, and the Enter key was pressed twice to create the space, taking up quite a bit more space on the page.

4 You can specify the way you want the spaces between characters to be measured. Either place your pointer in the paragraph you want to change, or select the text you want to manipulate, then choose Format, Spacing Between Characters. The Spacing Between Characters dialog box that displays gives you a number of choices: Very Tight; Tight; Loose; Very Loose.

Using Special Characters

Y ou can use special characters to dress up your text, add emphasis to your message, or just have fun during the process of creating a publication. Used judiciously these elements add flair and individuality. Fancy First Letters can be ornate or jaunty, and certainly draw the reader's eye to a paragraph. Symbols are sometimes necessary (such as the copyright or trademark symbols), and sometimes fun (a checkmark instead of a bullet adds flair to a checklist). Characters that are raised or lowered at the baseline add a professional touch, such as the "th" in a number (as in "this is the 99th time I've told you that").

The trick in using special characters is not to overdo it—you don't want your message to look like a ransom note.

TIP SHEET

▸ After you've inserted a fancy first letter, if you don't like it, place your pointer anywhere in the same paragraph and open the Format menu. You'll see that the menu item for this feature has changed to Change Fancy First Letter. You can pick a different style, customize the letter, or choose Remove to go back to the original font.

▸ When you're inserting symbols, many of the font names are hard (or impossible) to read. If you know which font you want to head for to get the symbol you need, choose it from the Text Format toolbar. When you go to the Insert menu to choose a symbol, that font will be displayed in the dialog box.

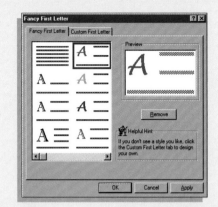

▶ **1** To create a fancy first letter, place your pointer anywhere in the paragraph that you want to begin with this letter and choose Format, Fancy First Letter. The dialog box shows you a number of different fancy styles. Select the one you like and click on OK.

**5th Floor Conference Room
Next to the H$_2$O Cooler**

6 After you've made your selection, choose OK. Publisher doesn't just move the characters into position, it reduces the size of the character to make it all work.

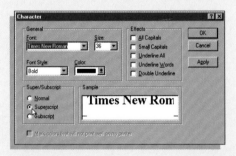

5 Superscript and subscript characters are occasionally needed, and when that happens it's easy to do. Select the characters you have to change and choose Format, Character from the menu bar. In the lower left side of the Character dialog box, select Superscript or Subscript.

2 If you don't see one you like, click the Custom First Letter tab on the dialog box to design your own. You can specify the position, font, size, color, and attributes. You can also indicate the number of letters in addition to the first letter of the paragraph that you want to manipulate in this way. Perhaps if the first word is a short one you'll want to make the whole word fancy.

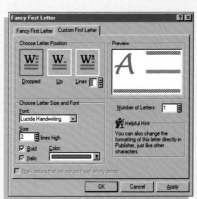

3 Publisher provides an enormous variety of special symbols you can place in a text frame. Just put the pointer where you want the symbol to appear and choose Insert, Symbol from the menu bar. The symbol font that displays in the Insert Symbol dialog box matches the font that is chosen at the cursor point. There's every chance you find many other interesting symbols, so click the arrow to the right of the Show Symbols From box and scroll through the choices.

4 When you find a font and a symbol you want to use, double-click on the symbol to place it into the document. You'll find that with many symbols, it's a good idea to select them after they're on your page and then select a larger font size. This illustration shows some of my own favorite symbol fonts.

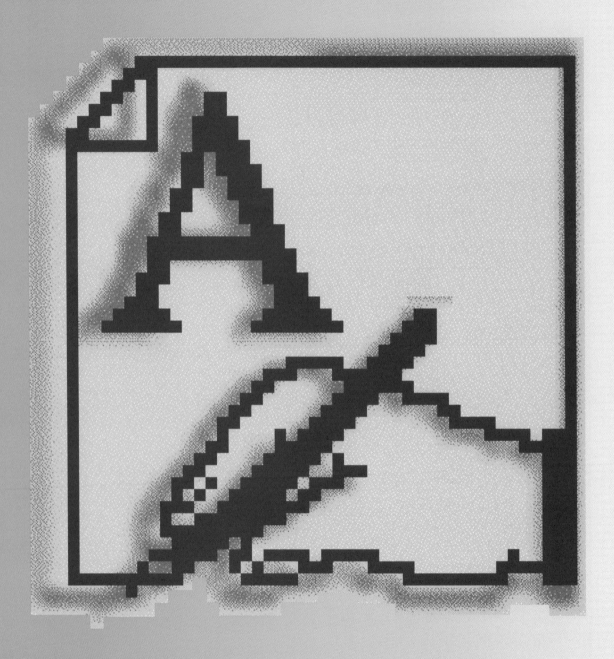

CHAPTER 9

How to Use Fancy Borders, Pattern Fills, and Gradients

Publisher offers two types of borders you can use to highlight frames or pages. There are line borders that can be applied in a variety of thicknesses and colors, as well as colorful artistic borders that add zest and style.

In this chapter you learn how to use line borders in a more creative way, styling the border instead of accepting the standard line on all four sides of your frame. You'll also learn how to put some spice into the background of your publication with the use of color fills.

How to Add a Border to a Frame

You can frame your work with a border that's ornate, spiffy, cool, or elegant. Your choice of style depends on your mood and the objects inside the border. Choosing to use a border means you've decided a frame or a page needs some decorating in order to make it stand out.

Applying the border is easy; it's the decision-making process that's difficult. That picture of your great-great-great-grandfather that's over the fireplace (the one where he's on his steed, holding his saber) needed a thick ornate frame (possibly gilded). But a charcoal drawing needs a thin, more subtle treatment when you frame it. The same thing is true of your frames and pages. Pick a border that does justice to your publication, but doesn't overwhelm its message.

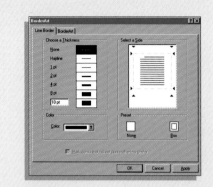

▶ **1** To put a fancy border on a frame, select the frame and click the Border button on the Format toolbar. Instead of clicking on a border line and applying a standard border around the frame, choose More from the drop-down menu.

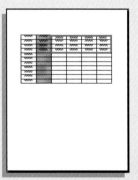

5 You can highlight parts of a table to emphasize the contents by placing a colorful border around the specific cells you want to draw attention to. Select the cells you want to use and then apply the border as described above.

TIP SHEET

▶ **You can use the choose-a-thickness-per-side feature of line borders to create your own drop shadow effect. Just make two adjacent sides very thick and a dark color.**

▶ **To remove a border, select the frame and choose None from the list that appears when you click the Border button on the Format toolbar.**

▶ **If you have a clip art frame in which you have set the properties to wrap text around the picture instead of the frame, line borders are placed around the outline shape of the picture (which rarely looks attractive).**

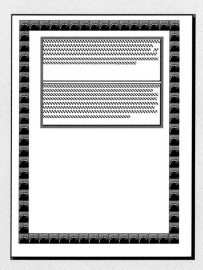

2 The Line Border tab of the BorderArt dialog box lets you create borders of various thicknesses and a variety of colors. You can make your borders a little more interesting by changing the thickness and color of specific sides of the frame. In the Select a Side box, click a side, then click on Border Thickness. You can have a different thickness for each of the four sides of the frame, or a different color for each of the four sides, or any permutation or combination of thickness and color. Choose OK when you have finished clicking away.

3 When you create a border for a frame that has text in columns, you can also make decisions about the border line between the columns. You can place a border line between columns by clicking on the vertical line between columns in the Select a Side box. Then select a border thickness and color.

 4 Borders for Table frames let you manipulate thickness and color for both the horizontal and vertical gridlines. Select either line in the Select a Side box and then choose a thickness and color. To make all the lines the same border style, select a thickness and color and then choose Grid.

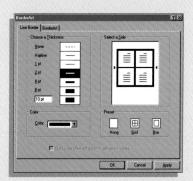

How to Add a Fancy Border to Multiple Frames or a Full Page

You can enhance the effect of borders by including more than one frame within a border, or bordering an entire page. And you don't have to stick to plain, dull, lines. You can use some of the fancy border art provided by Publisher.

Achieving this effect is a two-step process. You have to create the border's outline, then apply the border.

▶ ❶ To outline multiple frames or a whole page in order to place a border on the outline, click the Box tool on the Publisher toolbar.

 Click OK to apply the border to your page.

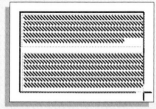

2 To put a box around multiple frames, place your pointer in the upper-left corner of the section you want to enclose. Drag the mouse down and to the right to create a box. This box is the entity that will have a border applied. You can use the sizing handles of the box to surround the multiple frames with exactly the right proportions.

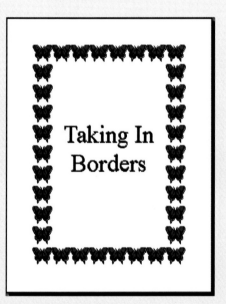

Taking In Borders

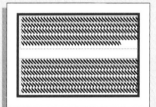

3 With the box selected, click the Borders tool on the Format toolbar and choose More. When the BorderArt dialog box opens you can select a line thickness and a color. Choose OK to apply your choice to the box.

4 To border a page with a fancy design, follow the same procedure, using the Box tool to enclose the entire page. Then select the Border tool and choose More. This time, click the BorderArt tab so you can add a fancy, graphic border to the page. Scroll through the choices until you find a design that matches your taste or whim.

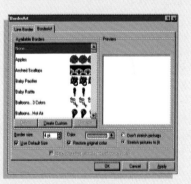

How to Use Gradient Fills and Patterns

Add even more zest to the appearance of your publication by using splashes of color to illuminate your message. Publisher provides a way to fill objects with colors and color patterns. Used judiciously, and with taste and common sense, this can make your publication extra special.

A pattern is a way to put texture into color, creating a more interesting eye-catcher than a plain color. It is, however, busier than plain color, so you won't want to use it on a busy frame. A gradient fill changes its depth and texture within the frame, creating an interesting and multidimensional effect. It actually is a graduated fill, moving from dense to thin in its application of dots of color.

▶ **1** To use a pattern in a frame, select the frame and then click on the Object Color button on the Format toolbar. When the drop-down menu appears, click on Patterns & Shading.

TIP SHEET

▶ When you're putting a pattern or a gradient fill behind a graphic frame, be careful about the choices you make. You don't want to lose the impact of the clip art by having the background overwhelm it.

▶ Even if you're not printing to a color printer, selecting a color will impact the levels of gray that your black and white printer produces. Picking pastel shades results in lighter shades of gray.

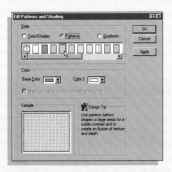

② Select the Patterns option button and scroll through the display to find a pattern you think suits the frame you're working on. Select suitable colors and choose OK to apply the pattern fill to the frame.

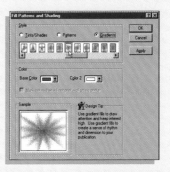

③ To use a gradient fill instead of a pattern, select the Gradients option button. Scroll through the choices to pick the pattern and shape you like, then choose OK to apply it to your frame.

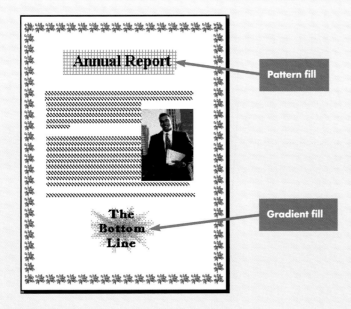

Annual Report

Pattern fill

The Bottom Line

Gradient fill

④ To create a pattern or gradient fill for multiple frames or a page, click the Box tool and draw a box around the elements or the page. Then choose the pattern and color scheme you want to use.

⑤ To give yourself a larger range of color choices, select the frame, click the Object Color button and choose More Colors.

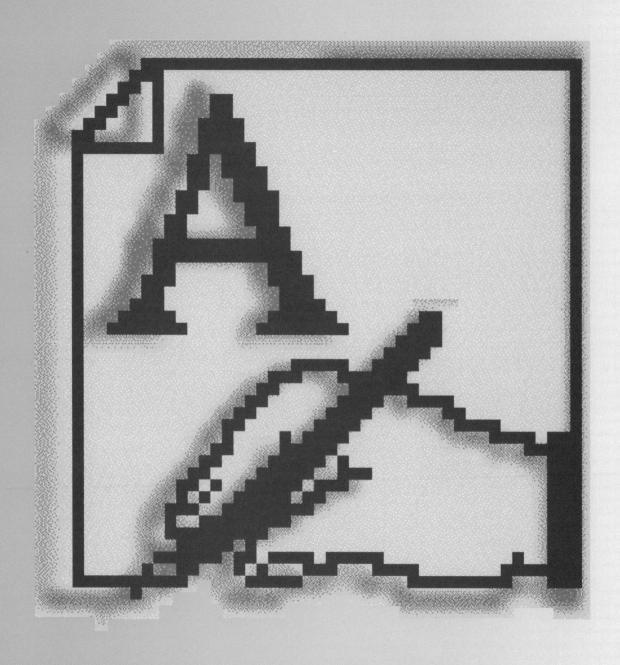

CHAPTER 10

How to Use Publisher's Advanced Graphics Capabilities

Publisher provides some truly amazing advanced capabilities to help you use graphics in a way that makes your presentation look professional and artistic (even if you aren't the least bit artistic and can't draw a happy face cartoon without a stencil).

You can use multiple graphics at the same spot on a page to create some eye-catching effects, and you can place a faint reproduction of a graphic across an entire page (or every page in your publication).

How to Layer Pictures for Special Effects

Layering is the process of moving one object over another object so that there is some overlap. In order for both objects to be seen, you don't want to cover either object completely, just overlap them in such a way as to create an interesting effect. You can layer graphics on graphics, or text on graphics.

As with other graphical effects available through Publisher's tools, *restraint* is the key word. Don't overdo it, or else you'll lose the advantage Publisher gives you of making your publication look as if it were produced by a professional graphics designer.

1 To layer graphics, create both graphic items on the same page. Select one of the graphic objects (the mouse pointer turns to a moving van) and drag it over the other graphic object.

6 To display the text on the graphic cleanly (without the background of the text box) you have to make the text frame transparent so the graphic shows through. Select the text frame and press Ctrl+T.

TIP SHEET

▶ The first time you put one object on top of another, Publisher offers to help you finish the task by showing you a demo on layering objects, or opening the Help files to give you step-by-step instructions. Choose the method of help you prefer, or choose Continue to do it without Publisher's assistance.

▶ One of the more interesting ways to layer objects is to layer shapes. More information about using shapes is found in Chapter 15.

2 If the graphic that is in the foreground should be behind the other graphic (as in the left page of this illustration), select it and click the Send To Back button on the Standard toolbar. When the graphic moves to the background, the effect you intended is achieved (check the right page of this illustration).

3 You aren't limited to two graphics when you want to use layering. You can use as many items as you need to in order to get the effect you want.

4 When you're layering multiple objects, there's more than the simple "front and back" layering movement available. You can move objects back one or more layers at a time (or move them forward one or more layers at a time) by selecting an object and using the options on the Arrange menu.

5 You can also move a text frame so that it is on top of a graphics frame.

How to Make a Watermark

A watermark is a faint imprint on paper, usually indicating the paper's brand name or rag content (hold your good letterhead bond up against the light and you should see its watermark). Watermarks are also applied to paper with software such as Publisher, sometimes to put a company logo on every page that's printed, or sometimes to indicate that a paper is confidential or even top secret.

When you apply a watermark, you work on the background of the page. The foreground remains free for placement of your text and graphics. When you print your publication, the watermark shows through the contents of the page. When you work on the background of a page, you're creating an element that will appear on every page of your publication. (There are ways to change or eliminate the background element for specific pages; more information about working with the background is available in Chapter 13.)

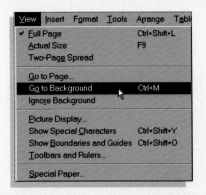

▶ **1** To create a watermark, you have to move to the background of a page in your publication. Choose View, Go To Background or press Ctrl+M.

6 If you cannot see the background graphic it means the element you're adding to the page is not transparent. Press Ctrl+T to make a frame transparent.

TIP SHEET

▶ **Watermarks must be graphical elements, so if you want to use text you have to use WordArt (see Chapter 15).**

▶ **If you're creating a full page watermark, when you insert the clip art, choose Change the Picture to Fit The Frame in order to guarantee the watermark covers the page.**

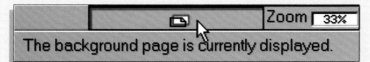

The background page is currently displayed.

2 When you are working on the background, everything you do is very much the same as when you're working on the foreground. In fact, it's hard to remember that you're creating background elements that will appear on every page. Publisher reminds you by changing the Page button on the Status Bar into an icon that shows a page lifted from its background.

3 To create a graphic for a watermark, begin with the normal process. Click the Picture tool on the Publisher toolbar and create a frame for the watermark. The frame can use any portion of the page, or all of the page. Right-click in the frame and choose Insert Clip Art, then pick the clip art you want to use as a watermark.

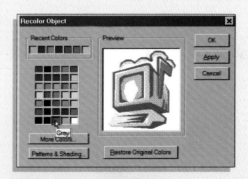

4 Right-click on the clip art and choose Recolor Object from the menu. Click the gray color button. Then choose OK. (You can also choose More Colors to see a palette with a variety of shades of gray.)

5 The watermark is on the background of the page and will appear on every page of your publication. Return to the foreground (use Ctrl+M or choose View, Go To Foreground) and begin adding elements to your publication.

How to Create a Custom Text Wrap Boundary

The way text wraps around graphical elements makes a big difference in the appearance of your publication. There are times when it's a good idea to let the text wrap around the frame, and other times when you want to integrate the graphic with the text a bit more by having the text wrap around the shape of the graphic instead of the rectangle of the frame.

You actually have more choices than wrapping to the frame or wrapping to the graphic. You can tweak the text wrap around a graphic in order to make the final effect more professional looking.

▶ **1** To customize text wrapping, you have to deal with the irregularities of the graphic element, and there are tools on the Formatting toolbar to help you accomplish this. When you wrap text to the frame, the Format toolbar contains a cropping tool (called the Crop Picture tool). When you wrap text to the graphic however, the Crop Picture tool goes away and is replaced by the Edit Irregular Wrap button.

5 If you want to ease the text wrap in or out in a particular spot, and there is no handle at that spot, you can create one. Position the pointer where you want to create a handle and hold down the Ctrl key. The pointer changes to an Add pointer. Click the mouse, and presto, you have a new handle.

TIP SHEET

▶ When you wrap text around a graphic, sometimes a few letters pop up on the opposite side of the graphic. While you can fix this by moving the graphic closer to the edge of the frame, it's slicker to move the handles on that side of the graphic in the direction of the frame. The characters will move back to the text side of the graphic.

▶ If you change your mind and want to undo the resizing, click the graphic. Then, in succession, click Wrap Text to Frame, followed by Wrap Text To Picture. Publisher asks if you want to have a new boundary created automatically. Answer Yes.

2 To change how text wraps around a graphic, click the graphic to select it, then make sure that Wrap Text to Picture is selected (click the Wrap Text To Picture button on the toolbar or select it from the Object Frame Properties dialog box). Then click the Edit Irregular Wrap button. This action displays a handle for every twist and turn in the graphic's shape, and in order to see it properly you should press F9 to zoom in.

3 Put your pointer on any handle until it changes to an Adjust pointer. Then drag the handle in the direction that's needed to change the way the text wraps around the graphic. This is a way to fine-tune and tweak the text wrap for this graphic.

Once upon a time, in a land far far away, a little girl named Sarah was waiting for her prince to come. Sarah was getting really disgusted with all the frogs she'd kissed. *Yuck!* She'd tried sleeping for a hundred years, but got wakeful and very restless after about 8 hours.

4 As you move handles in and out, the text wrap changes. If you've tightened the handles around the graphic, the text will weave in and out along the contours of the graphic shape. (Of course, you could also loosen the handles to keep the text away from the graphic, yet maintain the irregular wrap that comes with wrapping to the figure instead of the frame.)

Once upon a time, in a land far far away, a little girl named Sarah was waiting for her prince to come. Sarah was getting really disgusted with all the frogs she'd kissed. *Yuck!* She'd tried sleeping for a hundred years, but got wakeful and restless after about 8 hours. *Ar-rgh.*

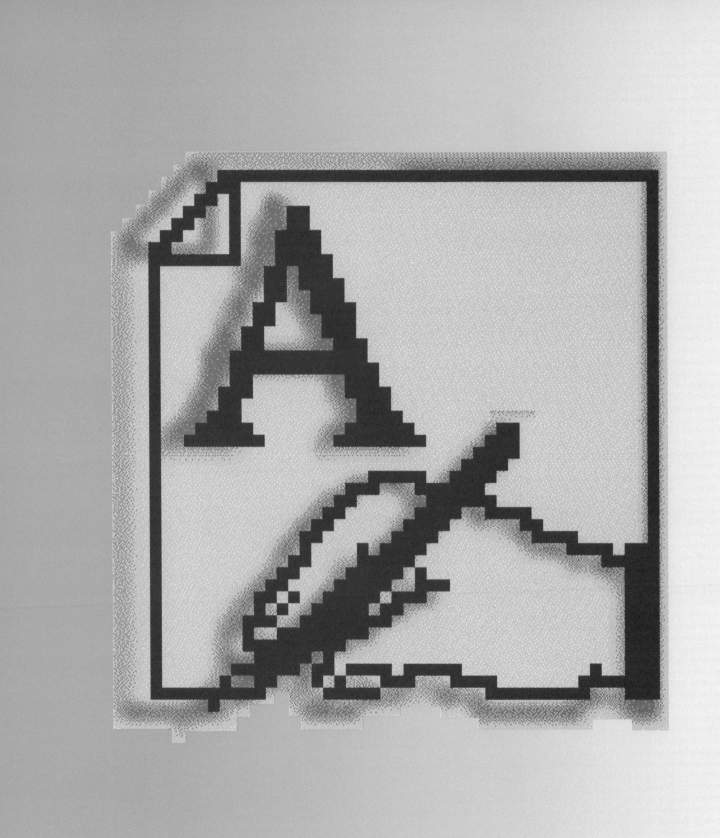

CHAPTER 11

How to Use Publisher's Special Text Features

Publisher provides a host of text tools to cover those special situations when you need text organized into something other than just paragraphs of information. Lists, both bulleted and numbered, are frequently needed and Publisher makes it easy to format text this way. You'll see all the possibilities in this chapter.

The spell checking tool is just what you need to save yourself a lot of embarrassment, and you'll learn how to use it in this chapter.

We'll also cover the steps needed to bring text into your publication from another software program, perhaps a word processor or a text editor.

How to Create Bullet and Number Lists

One of the best ways to make special information stand out on a page is to break it down into short sentences and print it with bullets next to each item. Sometimes special information is conveyed better by listing it by number. Perhaps you're giving instructions on how to accomplish something, or you're giving a list of choices for people to make.

You can have Publisher do all the formatting for you when you need these special devices, and you can even customize the way Publisher runs this automated feature.

When you create a list, each paragraph (begun each time you press Enter) begins a new list entity, either a new bulleted item or a new numbered item. You can create a list from scratch or select existing text and turn it into a list.

TIP SHEET

▶ If you don't want to use one of the bullet styles you see displayed, you can pick something totally different by choosing New Bullet. When the New Bullet dialog box appears, click the arrow to the right of the font box and choose a font from the list. Look for a font that seems to have a lot of interesting symbols (hint: try Wingdings). Then find a symbol you want to use as a bullet and double-click on it.

▶ If you've created a numbered list and you want to change its starting number, select the first numbered item and open the Indents and Lists dialog box. Enter the new number in the Start At box. Publisher will renumber that item and every item that follows it.

▶ **1** To create a bullet list, choose Format, Indents and Lists from the menu bar. When the Indents and Lists dialog box opens, choose Bulleted List. Then pick a bullet style from the choices displayed. You can also adjust the size of the indent of the line that's bulleted.

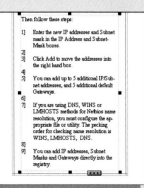

6 Sometimes when you create a list from existing text you have blank spaces between each section. Publisher saw that the Enter key was pressed and added a number. Don't worry, just place your cursor on the line with the number that has no text and press Del. Publisher will renumber the following list entries automatically. Repeat this for each blank numbered line.

2 If you specified a bullet list before you began entering text, a bullet appears each time you press Enter and the first character you type is indented by the interval you specified. If you selected existing text before you applied the bullet feature, that text is reformatted into a bulleted list.

3 For a shortcut to creating bullets, you can use the Bulleted or Numbered List button on the Format toolbar. Click a bullet style to begin entered bulleted text or to convert existing text that you've selected first. If you choose More, the Indents and Lists dialog box appears.

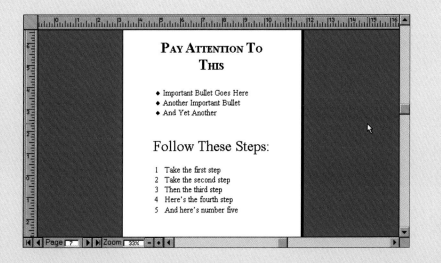

5 You can configure the way you want your numbered list to appear. Choose numbers or letters as the Format; choose a character to appear after the number as a Separator (the choices include period, colon, parentheses, and brackets); choose a starting number if this list isn't supposed to start at number 1 (you may be breaking up the list with paragraphs and want to start each section where the last section left off).

4 To create a numbered list, the steps are similar to those used to create a bulleted list. Either place the pointer at the spot in the text frame where you want to begin a numbered list, or select existing text that you want to turn into a numbered list. Then choose Format, Indents and Lists and select Numbered List.

How to Use Spell Checking

One of the real blessings of using Publisher is that after you create a slick, professional publication with all the graphics placed perfectly, and all the headlines and text looking as if they were typeset, you don't have to be embarrassed by a word that's misspelled.

The Publisher spell check works similarly to spell checkers in word processors. If it finds a word in your story that isn't in its dictionary, it alerts you. If there is a similar word it will suggest that perhaps you might have wanted to use that word.

▶ **1** To check the spelling of a story, first select the first text frame for the story, then press F7 (or click the Spelling button on the Standard toolbar). The spell check is performed on that story and the first word that's found that is not in the spelling dictionary is displayed.

TIP SHEET

▶ **If you have not used the overflow text feature to continue a story onto another frame, the spell check doesn't know where the story goes and will stop at the end of the frame.**

▶ **The spell check ignores words that have numbers in them.**

2 If you spelled the word incorrectly and Publisher displays the correct spelling of the word in the Change To box, choose Change. If you think the word will occur again (misspelled again), choose Change All so you don't have to go through the step each time. If you're sure the word is what you meant to type and you don't want to correct it this time, choose Ignore. If the word occurs again, it will be displayed again. To have the spell checker ignore the word every time it occurs while you are performing this spell check, choose Ignore All. If the word is correct and you will be using it frequently, add it to the spell checker's dictionary by choosing Add. Hereafter, it won't be challenged. This is usually used for proper names or technical terms that you use often.

I kant spel too gud
but I dont haf to
werry about it with
the spel cheker

3 Sometimes the spell checker offers a number of choices for the correct word. Click on the one that's the word you meant to type, and that word moves to the Change To box. Then click Change.

4 When the story has been checked, Publisher asks if you want to have other stories checked. If you choose Yes, all the stories in your publication will be checked for spelling.

5 It's a good idea to select Ignore Words in UPPERCASE, because most of the time the words aren't in the spell check dictionary. They're usually abbreviations (for example, for state names) or acronyms.

How to Use Text from Other Programs

There is no reason to retype text that already exists in another software package. One of the advantages of using Windows is being able to use the clipboard. You can copy text from one program onto the clipboard and then paste the clipboard's contents into your publication.

If you've stored documents in a word processor, or in one of the text editors that comes with Windows, you can bring all or part of the contents into your publication with a few clicks of the mouse.

1 To begin, open the software application that has the text you want to bring into your publication. Then use the appropriate keystrokes or mouse movements to open the document that contains the text you need.

5 You can even grab text from a DOS session on your Windows 95 computer. Use the menu system available from the DOS window to tell the operating system you want to Mark text. Use the mouse to highlight the text, then press Enter to copy it, move to your text frame, and paste it.

TIP SHEET

▶ If you are going to be pasting multiple sections of text between another program and Publisher, open both programs, resize the program windows so you can see both of them on your screen, and move between them quickly.

▶ You can copy and paste text between two separate publications by opening a second copy of Publisher and opening the source publication in it. To open another copy of Publisher, just use the same steps you used to open the copy of Publisher you're currently working in. Publisher will let you do this as long as both copies of the software don't try to load the same publication document.

2 Select the text you want to bring into your publication. Then press Ctrl+C to copy the text to the Clipboard.

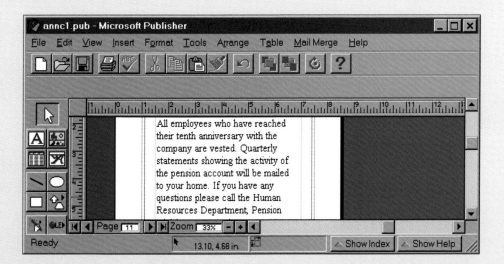

3 Move to the text frame in your publication that will receive the text. Place your pointer at the appropriate point and press Ctrl+V to paste the text into your publication. If all the text doesn't fit into the frame, create another text frame on a different page and put the overflow text into it. (See Chapter 7 to refresh your memory about putting overflow text into additional frames.)

4 You can also pick up text from applications other than word processors or text processors. If you receive an e-mail message with information you want to put into your publication, select it, copy it to the Clipboard, and paste it into a text frame.

TRY IT!

Now that you have increased your skill level, you can try creating a more complicated publication. The fact that it's more complex won't make it more difficult, because the things you learned in the last few chapters give you the tools you need to make short work of tasks that seem a bit intricate.

In this exercise you'll create a small newsletter you can use to distribute the company gossip throughout your organization, or a newsletter you can send to family and friends in order to keep them up on the news from your household. As you go through the steps, the chapter that covered the information is noted for you in case you want to go back and refresh your knowledge.

1 With a new blank document in the Publisher window, create a text frame for the title at the top of the page by clicking the Text tool on the Publisher toolbar and dragging your mouse on the page until the frame is the desired size. *Chapter 2.*

Enter the text for the title, then select the text, center it, and change the font size so it is fairly large.
Click the Object Color button to put a pattern or gradient fill in the title frame. *Chapter 9.*

Draw a text frame below the title frame to fill the rest of the page. Right-click on the frame and select Text Frame Properties. Change the number of columns to 2. Then click OK.

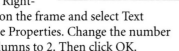

Click the Border tool on the Format toolbar, then choose More. Choose a border width, then choose Grid to place lines between your columns. Click OK. *Chapter 9.*

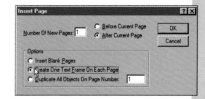

Choose Insert, Page from the menu bar.
Insert one page and choose Create One Text Frame on Each Page, then choose OK. This exercise is for a two-page newsletter, but if you're ambitious and want to try a four-page newsletter you should insert three additional pages with text frames. Use the right-click menu to set this page up for two columns and then create the same Grid border you did for the first page.

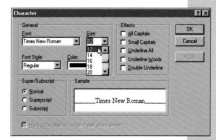

Return to your first page and click on the text frame to select it.
Choose Format, Character and pick a font and a size for the newsletter text and click OK.

Begin entering text. If you already have a newsletter story written in a word processor, bring it into your newsletter. To do so, open the software application that has the text and use the appropriate commands to open the document that contains the text you need. Select the text and press Ctrl+C to copy it to the clipboard. *Chapter 11.*

Continue to next page ▶

 TRY IT!

Continue below

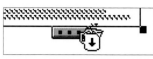

 8

Click the Publisher button on the task bar to return to Publisher. Click the text box and press Ctrl+V to paste the document into your newsletter. *Chapter 11.*

9

Continue to enter text and/or import it to fill your newsletter with all the stories you want to cover. When your text overfills the frame, Publisher asks if you want to have your text automatically flow to another frame. You can choose Yes to have Publisher do this, or choose No to control the flow of text between frames yourself. I always choose No so I can handle the task myself. *Chapter 7.*

10

To move the overflow text into the text frame you created on the next page, click the Connect button at the bottom of the frame (which has three dots to indicate there is overflow text). The mouse pointer turns into a pitcher. *Chapter 7.*

11

Click in the text frame on the next page to have the pitcher pour the overflow text in. Notice that the button at the top of the frame has an arrow pointing back to the page where the story started.

12

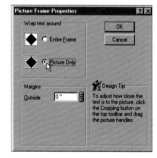

Now let's add some flair to the newsletter. We'll start by adding some graphic elements to spice up the page. Return to the first page and create a picture frame anywhere on the page, then insert clip art. Right-click the frame and choose Picture Frame Properties. Specify that you want to wrap text around the Picture Only, then choose OK. *Chapter 6.*

13

I like to save some space on the page at the end of the newsletter for information about the publication. You can use this to tell people how to contact you, how to submit stories, or take care of mundane company business. This section usually takes special formatting, so I usually create a separate text frame for it.

14

Create a special border for the new text frame. Click the Border tool, choose More, and move to the Border-Art tab. Select the border design you like, then choose OK.

15

For this section, add the rules for submitting stories to the newsletter. Enter the introductory text. Enter each rule, then select that text. (You may have additional text after the rules.) Click the Bulleted or Numbered List tool and select a bullet style. If you want to make this a numbered list, choose More and specify that this is a numbered list when the dialog box appears.

16

To make the newsletter a bit more interesting visually, you can add a watermark. Move to the background by pressing Ctrl+M. Then create a picture frame (you can make it as large as you wish, including as large as the page). Choose a clip art picture that fits the mood of your newsletter. *Chapter 10.*

17

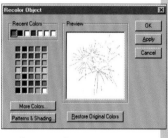

Right-click on the clip art and choose Recolor Object from the menu. Then choose grey or silver to create a neutral tone. Choose OK.

18

Press Ctrl+M to move back to the foreground. Select each frame in your newsletter and press Ctrl+T to make it transparent so you can see the watermark through the text. (Actually, I don't usually make the graphics frames transparent, preferring to have them print cleanly.) *Chapter 10.*

19

Avoid embarrassment! Run a spell check on the document. Select the first text frame and press F7. When the spell check for the story is complete, Publisher will offer to check the rest of the publication. Answer Yes. *Chapter 11.*

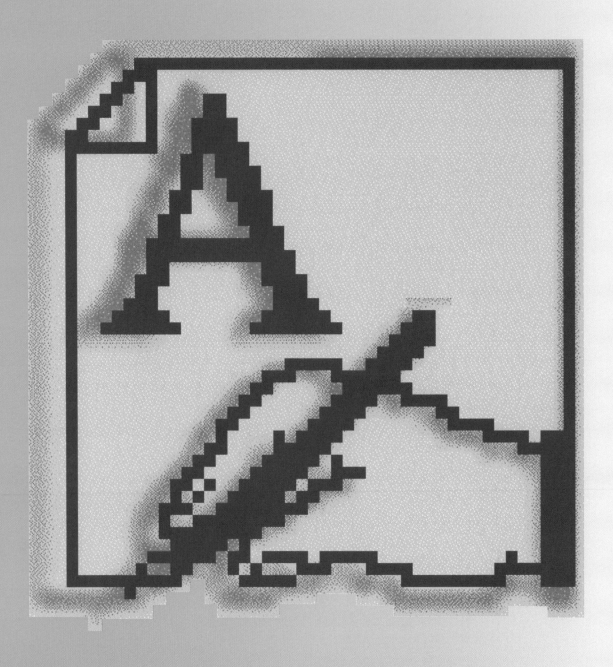

CHAPTER 12

Aligning, Nudging, Grouping, and Layering

Everything you place on a page doesn't have to divide the page into little square areas—that's so predictable and boring. You can move the elements around so they're "just so." This will create a unique, more interesting appearance for your publication.

In this chapter you'll learn how to maneuver frames around, above, below, on top of, and beneath each other. You'll also learn how to group objects so that moving one moves the others.

How to Align and Nudge Objects on the Page

L ining up the objects on a page is one of the most important steps you take as you fine-tune your publication. Lining up doesn't mean that each frame has to be spaced equally apart from all the other frames in a neat set of rows. It means that things that are associated with each other should fall into a pattern that makes the association obvious.

In order to accomplish this, you can line up objects so that they're aligned with a margin or a guide, or perhaps are just lined up with each other, matching each other's positions on the page.

▶ **①** Once you've put a few objects on a page, you may decide you want to "neaten up" the page by lining them up. The objects in this illustration have no particular arrangement and look amateurish. As other objects are added, it will be hard to tell which objects are related to each other, or which objects are paired.

TIP SHEET

▶ **If the objects you want to arrange are not contiguous, move everything around so you can get a box around all the objects you want to use.**

▶ **If you've grouped objects and then change your mind, click anywhere on the Publisher window outside the page, and the box around the objects will disappear.**

2 If you want to line up objects on a page, they must be contiguous so that they can all be enclosed within a box. One way to enclose contiguous objects in a box is to select them and let Publisher create the box for you. To do that, hold down the Ctrl key while you select each object you want to include. A grey box surrounds the selected objects. At the bottom of the grey box is a Group button, indicating that the objects within the box are considered a group.

3 You can also draw your own box around the obejcts. Click the Pointer tool on the Publisher toolbar and place your pointer on the outside edge of the first object you want to include. Then hold down the left mouse button and drag the mouse until you've included all the objects you need.

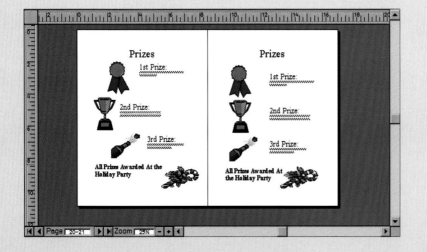

4 When you draw your own box, the only objects that join the group are those that fall entirely within the lines of the box. If only a portion of an object is within the box, it will not be included in the group. This means you don't have to worry about moving extraneous objects entirely out of the way.

5 Once the objects have been grouped, you can line them up. Choose Arrange, Line Up Objects to begin working with the elements, using the Line Up Objects dialog box.

How to Align and Nudge Objects on the Page (Continued)

Once the Line Up Objects dialog box is displayed, you can begin to line up the objects by using the available choices. Note the sample display in the middle of the dialog box, which will help you visualize the effect of each choice on the way the objects on your page line up.

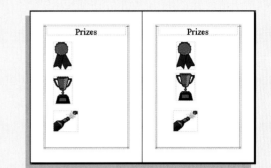

▶ **6** Use the Left to Right section of the dialog box if you want to maneuver the objects using a horizontal reference. That means, for example, you can choose Left Edges to tell Publisher that you want to line up the objects so that their left sides are all at the same place on the page. The left side of the object farthest left becomes the standard, and the left side of the other objects line up so that the left sides of all objects are in exactly the same place. If you choose Center, the average location of the center of each object is calculated and all objects are lined up so their center points are at that location. Those two choices are illustrated in this figure. You can also choose to line the objects up along their right edges.

TIP SHEET

▸ You can't line up objects along their centers and along a margin at the same time.

▸ Since there is no diagonal arrow on your keyboard, when you are nudging an object and want to move it diagonally you have to alternate between an up/down arrow and a left/right arrow as you hold down the Alt key.

7 The Top to Bottom section of the dialog box offers similar choices, except everything is done in relation to the top and bottom of the page, and the top and bottom of the objects' frames. You can choose to line up objects along the top of their frames, the center of their frames (both of which are seen in this illustration), or the bottom of their frames.

8 If you want to line up the objects so they all have the same edge at the same place, and you also want to make sure that edge is along a margin, check the Align Along Margins choice on the dialog box.

Top row of graphics are lined up along bottom edge

Bottom row of text frames are lined up along top edge

Each top/bottom combination is lined up along the center of the frames

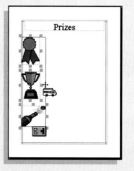

9 When objects have been lined up and you want to move them over or up or down, the box you enclose them in can be moved so that any manipulation affects all of them. That means you won't undo the work you just did to line them up against each other's edges.

10 Sometimes there's a frame that is almost in the right position, but not exactly where you want it. Every time you move it with your mouse, you overshoot your mark, or you move just a bit too far up or over. Using the mouse isn't the easiest approach to moving an object in tiny steps. The solution is to nudge the object into the perfect position. To nudge, select the object and move it in teeny steps by holding down the Alt key while you use the arrow keys to move it.

How to Group Objects

When you've created objects that belong together, you can ensure that whatever you do to one you do to the others. If the objects are meant to be stacked vertically and need to be moved over a bit, if they move as a group you don't have to manipulate them one at a time and you don't have to worry about the relationships changing.

▶ **1** To create a group, click the Selection tool on the Publisher toolbar and drag your mouse to draw a box around all the objects you want to place in the group. When the box is around the objects, a group button appears at the bottom. Note that the two connectors of that button are separated.

2 Click the group button to connect its two parts. Now your group is firmly connected and you can begin to manipulate the objects as a group. Notice that the group box has its own sizing handles.

3 You can resize every object in the group by using the group box handles to resize the group.

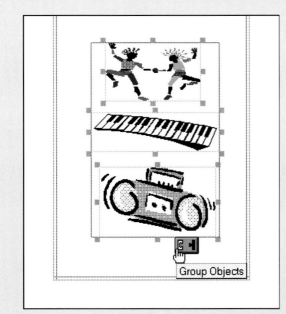

Group Objects

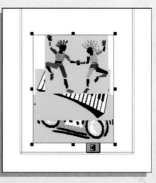

4 If you use the Object Color tool on the Formatting toolbar, the color of all the objects in the group changes. The same thing is true of borders, so that selecting a border for the group really places that border on each of the objects in the group.

5 You can also move or rotate the group to change the position of all the objects at the same time.

How to Change the Order of Layered Objects

S ome objects that belong together overlap each other. When that happens those objects are considered to be layered. The first object you create is on the bottom layer, the next is placed on top of the first, the next on top of the second, and so on. You work from the bottom up as you add objects.

You can change the appearance of the objects and the overall effect of the layered group by moving any individual object to another layer. This is sometimes an effective way to change the message your graphics are sending.

▶ **1** To layer objects, either create them so that they overlap or move existing objects over each other. The order in which you work determines the layer for each object.

6 You can layer a text frame over a graphic frame, which means, of course, that you'll have to make sure the text frame is always on top.

2 Once the layered objects are all on the page you can begin to manipulate the layers. You can resize and/or move any object. Selecting the object does not move it to the top of the layer—it stays in its current layer while you manipulate it.

3 When you want to move an object to another layer, select it. If you want this object to be at the bottom or the top of the layer, the quick way to accomplish this is to click the appropriate button on the Standard toolbar. Choose Send To Back or Bring To Front, depending on how you want to manipulate this object.

4 To move an object up or down one layer at a time, first select the object. Then choose Send Farther to move it back one layer from its present location, or Bring Closer to move it up one layer.

5 If you have a lot of layered objects, you can change the layering of more than one of them at a time. Create a group for several objects by clicking on each object while holding down the Ctrl key. That group will keep its own relative layering within itself, but you can change the layering of the group (relative to the other layered objects on the page) by using the commands explained above.

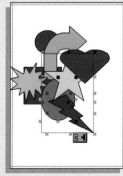

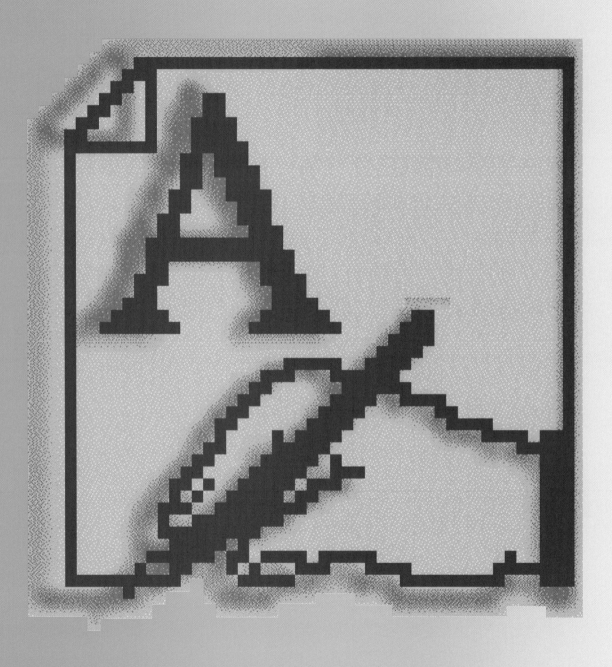

CHAPTER 13

Working with Your Publication's Background

When you were a child, did you have one of those plastic gizmos with a stylus? You wrote or drew on the plastic and then when you lifted the plastic sheet, everything disappeared. The plastic sat on a solid color background (usually black or grey). If you can visualize the toy, think about the effect of painting a red rose on the background. No matter what you drew on the plastic, you'd see the rose. You'd even see the rose when your plastic drawing surface was empty.

Your publication has a background too, and like that toy, whatever you put on it comes through whatever you've placed on your pages.

In this chapter you'll learn how to use the background to insert elements you want to see on every page of your publication.

How to Insert Page Numbers and Dates

Some publications, such as newsletters, booklets, or other multipage documents, need page numbering or dates, or both. If you use a word processor, you're probably familiar with using headers or footers to insert these elements so that they appear on every page. In Publisher, you can use the background of the pages of your publication to accomplish the same thing.

However, there is a very large difference between the way headers and footers work in word processors and the way backgrounds work in Publisher. Word processors adjust the page to make room for the headers and footers. Publisher does not. The background is its own page and the only way to use text on the background and have it seen on the page is to clear a spot for it on the page. You have to plan for text backgrounds. Graphic backgrounds (discussed in the next section) are easier to create and they're easier to make visible.

TIP SHEET

▶ When you're preparing your pages to make room for the background text elements, use a Ruler or Layout guide to be consistent (see Chapter 5 for more information about using guides).

▶ If you don't want your page number to be seen on the front page of your publication, create a blank text frame on that page directly over the text frame on the background. Make sure it's not transparent and it will hide the background text box.

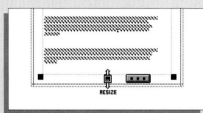

▶ **1** To insert page numbers or dates on every page of your publication, first decide where you want the element to fall on the page. Then make sure all the pages of your publication are blank in that spot. For instance, if you want to place a page number at the bottom of every page, make sure the bottom of every frame is above that spot.

7 Press Ctrl+M to return to your publication page and see the results. Remember that whatever you place on a background page will be seen on every page of your publication.

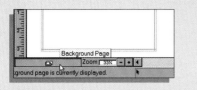

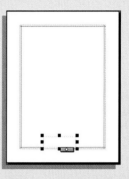

2 From any page in your publication, move to the background by pressing Ctrl+M. If you started from a blank page, the background page won't look different. Check the status bar—if you're on a foreground page you'll see the page number and the page controls, if you're on the background you'll see a double box.

3 To insert either the page number or the date, create a small text box on the background page.

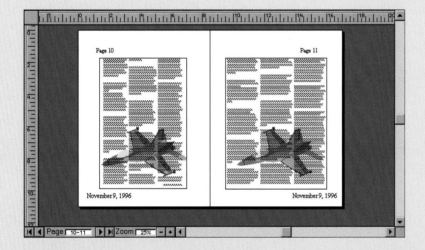

4 To insert a page number, make sure the text frame is selected and choose Insert, Page Numbers from the menu bar. A pound sign appears in the text box. The pound sign is the symbol for a page number on a background page.

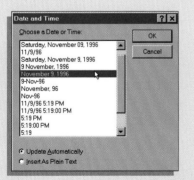

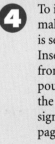

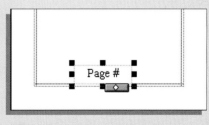

5 You can add additional words to the page text frame. Perhaps you might want to add the word "Page" or the letter P. You can also select the text and change the font, size, alignment, or attributes.

6 To insert a date, make sure the text frame is selected and choose Insert, Date or Time from the menu bar. Then choose the date format you want to use. Select Update Automatically if you want the date to change to reflect the current date every time you open this publication. Select Insert as Plain Text if you want today's date to be the permanent date on this publication.

How to Insert Graphics and Text onto the Background

S ince the objects you place on the background are seen on every page of your publication, this is a nifty way to decorate every page quickly. You can use your imagination to design all sorts of things, and in this section you'll learn about the steps needed to implement your ideas.

It's not uncommon to see an abstract graphic at the top or bottom of every page of a publication. Annual reports, handbooks, instructional guides, and other business publications use this device frequently. The basic rule of thumb is that strong graphics on the background will be seen through text on the page, but text on the background shows through only if you make room for it on the page.

TIP SHEET

▶ If you're not printing in color, you can select a color for a background graphic that will have just the level of grey you need, or you can specifically choose a shade of grey.

▶ Don't forget you can also dress up every page of your publication by adding a watermark to the background. See Chapter 10 for more information about watermarks.

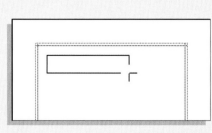

▶ **1** To place a color shape on every page of your publication, move to the background by pressing Ctrl+M. Then select a shape from the Publisher toolbar and drag your mouse to place it on the background. In this illustration, the Box tool is used to create a rectangle that is placed at the top of the background page.

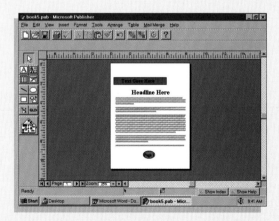

6 Press Ctrl+M to move back to the foreground. The graphics and text you've placed in the background show on every page (be sure to use Ctrl+T to make your foreground text frames transparent).

To add color to the shape, make sure it is selected, then click the Object Color button on the Format toolbar. Select a color and choose OK.

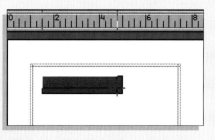

To add text on top of the color shape, click the Text tool on the Publisher toolbar and draw a frame over the color shape. If the shape is irregular, draw a text frame that fits within the color shape.

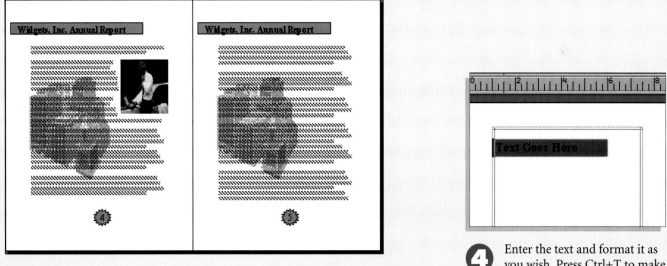

 Enter the text and format it as you wish. Press Ctrl+T to make this text frame transparent and allow the color shape behind it to show through.

Continue to add graphic shapes (with or without text) to the background, as needed.

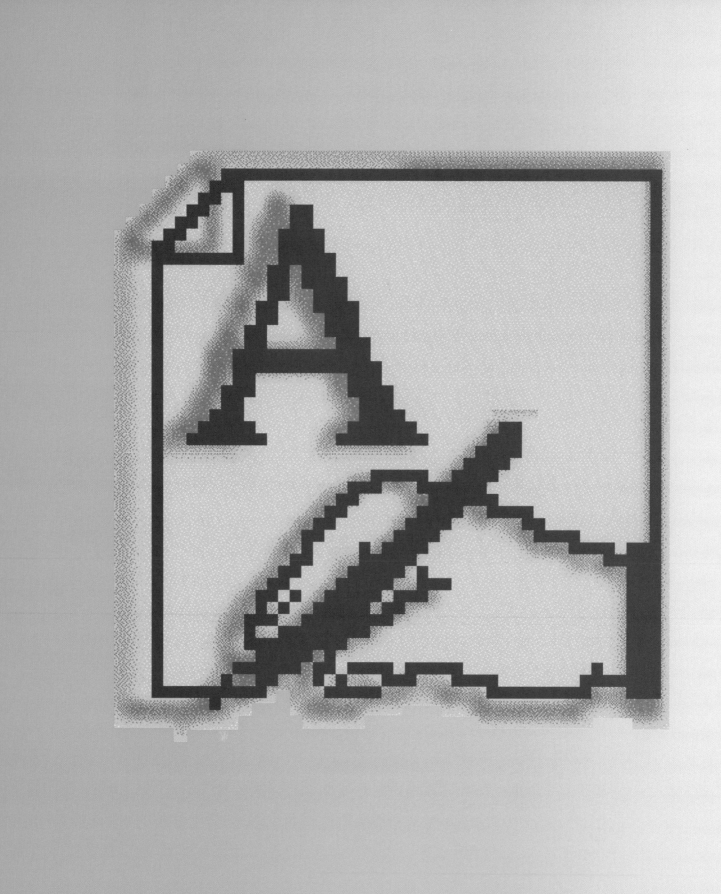

CHAPTER 14

Using Design Gallery and PageWizard

Publisher offers a couple of features that let you bring the talents of a professional designer to your work as you create a publication. The Publisher Design Gallery is filled with ornamental elements that can enhance the appearance of your work. Additionally, there's plenty of opportunity to add your own work to the gallery.

The PageWizard is a way to put a mini-document into your publication when you have a particular need for one of the special elements it provides.

In this chapter you'll learn how to browse and select the special objects available through these two powerful features.

How to Use Design Gallery to Add Flair to Your Publication

Stroll through the Publisher Design Gallery to see a wide variety of artwork you can use to add an extra, professional touch to your publication. The ornamental designs are similar to those you've seen in work produced by professional graphic artists.

▶ **1** To add an element from the Design Gallery to your publication, click the Design Gallery tool on the Publisher toolbar.

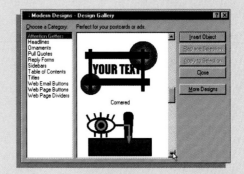

6 Use the scroll bar to scroll through the designs in the category until you find one you like.

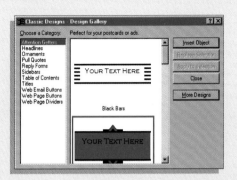

2 The Design Gallery window opens with a list of categories and a variety of designs for each category. The title bar displays the type of designs in this Gallery (in this case, Classic Designs).

3 You can choose another gallery by clicking More Designs.

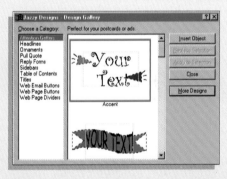

4 When you move to another gallery, you'll see that the design elements have a different look, a different personality. Find the gallery that matches the look you want for your publication.

5 When you decide on the gallery you want to use, choose the category you need for the element you're ready to add to your page.

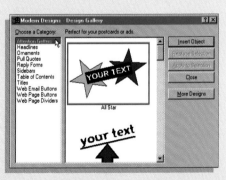

How to Use Design Gallery (Continued)

O nce you have found a gallery that has the style you're looking for, you can begin adding elements from the gallery to your publication. However, each element you add can be from a different gallery. Some of the galleries mix and match quite well, others don't. It's probably not a good graphic decision to put a classic design element next to a jazzy design element, but designs that are from the Jazzy and Modern galleries frequently work well together.

 7 Once you've decided on a design element, double-click it to place it on your page.

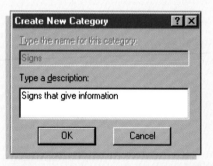

12 The category you assign is a new category for this new gallery you're building. Enter a description for the category. The description will appear on the Design Gallery window when you use this gallery. Click OK when you are finished.

8 Most of the design elements in the Design Gallery are multiple frames that have been grouped. You can see the group button displayed at the bottom of the frame. When you resize and move the design element to put it in its proper place, all the frames move together. You can also separate the groups and make changes to the size or position of individual frames. Then group the frames again. For information about working with groups, read Chapter 12.

9 If you design an element by yourself and you think you might want to use it again in other publications, you can add it to the Design Gallery. Start by clicking on your design to select it.

10 Click the Design Gallery tool and when the Design Gallery window opens, chose More Designs. Notice that there's an additional choice on the list— Add Selection to Design Gallery. Choose that option.

11 Publisher displays a notice telling you that you currently have a gallery open and you cannot add items to Publisher's galleries. You are asked if you want to start a new design set (which is a gallery). Answer Yes. The Adding an Object dialog box opens so you can give this design a name and assign it a category. Then choose OK.

How to Use Design Gallery (Continued)

Once you've created your own designs and saved them in a gallery, you can retrieve one whenever you need it. Besides explaining how to do that, this section covers some of the other elements available in the Design Gallery that you might find useful.

▶ **13** To bring a design you saved into a publication, click the Design Gallery tool and choose More Designs. Then choose Other Designs from the drop-down menu.

TIP SHEET

▶ **To replace the text in a Design Gallery element, you have to double click the individual text frame within the group. Most of the text in the Design Gallery is WordArt. To learn how to change text in a WordArt frame, read Chapter 15.**

▶ **Remembering the name of the publication that had a design you saved can get confusing once you've created and saved a lot of your own designs. I find it easier to create a publication specifically for designs. After I create and save a design in a "real" publication, I open the design-only publication, insert the new design, then save it again using my design publication. That's the one I choose whenever I want to hunt for my own work.**

▶ **When you ungroup designs from the Design Gallery in order to change them, you may find that one of the elements is also a group. Don't be surprised if you have to click at least one more group button to get down to the individual elements in the design.**

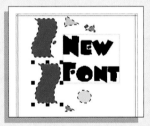

18 Once you've separated the elements you can eliminate one (or more) of them, change colors, change fonts, rearrange the way they're put together, or do all of that.

14 When the Other Designs dialog box opens, you'll see all your publications (you'll probably see some other files and folders, also, depending upon where you're saving your publication files). Since the designs you save are put into a gallery with the same name as the publication from which you took them, you just have to choose the publication that has the design you need.

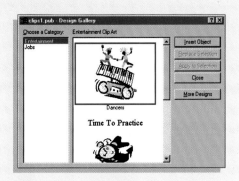

15 When the Design Gallery opens, the designs you saved, sorted by the categories you named, are available so you can place them into your next publication.

Fill Out and Return

PAYMENT METHOD

◇ AMERICAN EXPRESS   ◇ MASTERCARD

◇ VISA   ◇ DISCOVER

◇ CHECK ENCLOSED   ◇ DINER'S CLUB

ACCOUNT NUMBER

SIGNATURE

EXPIRATION DATE

BULK RATE CAR-RT SORT U.S. POSTAGE PAID (CITY, STATE) PERMIT NO. (XXX)	PRESORTED FIRST-CLASS MAIL U.S. POSTAGE PAID (CITY, STATE) PERMIT NO. (xxx)	FORTH-CLASS U.S. POSTAGE PAID (CITY, STATE) PERMIT NO. (XXX)

16 Besides the decorative and fancy design elements in the Design Gallery, there are several useful images, including forms for credit card purchases, and even graphics you can place on mailings for your special postage.

17 You can change any of the designs you select and then save them as if they were an original design. Many of the designs are really groups. You can click on various elements to determine the boundaries of the individual elements in the design. Click the group button to ungroup the elements so you can manipulate them.

How to Use PageWizard for Special Elements

There are some elements needed occasionally that you could design and create yourself, but it would take quite some time. Publisher has a built-in feature called PageWizard that does the hard work for you when you want to add one of these frames (a calendar, an advertisement, a coupon, or a logo). You get to make the design decisions, but you don't have to do all the work.

The PageWizard elements are multiple frames that have been grouped together to form the final object, so you can fine-tune them by manipulating the individual frames.

▶ **1** To use the PageWizard, click the PageWizard tool on the Publisher toolbar, then select the element you want to use.

6 For a logo, the style, the shape, the contents (a picture or initials), and text including a slogan are all part of the available design elements.

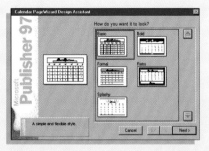

2 Move to the page and put your pointer at the position where you want the upper-left corner of the element to appear. Then press and hold the mouse button while you drag down and right until you have the size you want. When you release the mouse button, the PageWizard window appears. Each PageWizard starts by asking you to select a style. Click the style you like and then click Next.

3 The answers you give and the decisions you make depend upon the element you're adding. For a calendar, you must decide whether you want to spell out the days of the week or use abbreviations; and whether you want to have room for note-writing in the date blocks; whether you want the weeks to begin on Sunday or Monday.

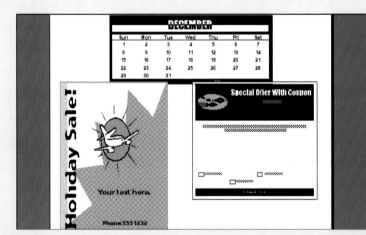

4 For an ad, you can pick the type of ad (classified, product, sale). Publisher will even give you a list of catchy phrases to use if your imagination fails you.

5 If you're inserting a coupon in your publication, you can choose whether it's a mailed-in coupon or a hand-it-over coupon; you can have an expiration date; and you can design the border and title.

TRY IT!

This is a good time to create a publication that incorporates some of the features you've learned about in the last couple of chapters. You can follow along to create a brochure that's designed to be mailed out to customers. As you go through the steps, we've indicated which chapter covered the information so you can refer back to that chapter if you need to refresh your memory.

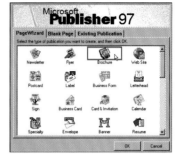

If you're already working in Publisher, choose File, Create New Publication to bring up the PageWizard. If you're just starting Publisher, it shows up automatically. Choose Brochure and click OK.

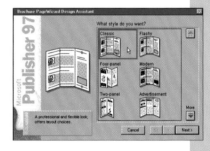

Choose a Classic three-panel brochure and click Next.

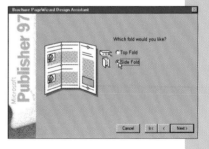

Select a side fold for the brochure, then click Next.

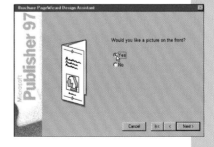

Opt for a picture on the front and click Next.

5

Let's have a balanced mixture of text and pictures. Choose Some text, some pictures.

6

We'll plan on leaving space for a mailing label. Choose Mail.

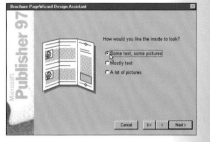

7

Move through the next couple of pages, reading the explanation of how brochures are laid out, then click Create It to tell the PageWizard to put together the framework for this brochure. When the PageWizard asks if you want step-by-step help as you create your brochure, answer Yes if you want the Help system opened. Answer No if you want to try it yourself.

8

Your brochure layout is ready and the first page is displayed in the Publisher window.

9

Click the right arrow in the Page section of the Status bar to look at the second page. This is not really a separate page, of course, because it will be printed on the back of the first page.

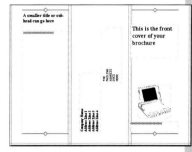

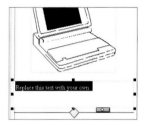

10

Click the text box on the front panel of the brochure and press F9 to zoom in on it.

11

Enter your own text and format it to your taste. In this case, the text is centered and bold. After you've entered the text, press F9 to zoom back out. *Chapter 3.*

12

Move to the middle panel and zoom in on the return address text frame. Replace the sample text with a real name and address. Tilt your head to see what you're typing. (It takes a few seconds to get used to maneuvering the arrow keys correctly as you move around the text frame.) Zoom back out when you're finished.

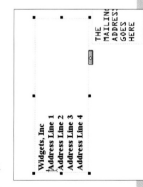

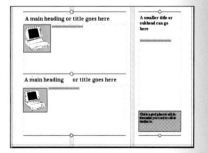

Continue to next page ▶

TRY IT!

**Continue
below**

Let's put a coupon
on the back panel
of this page. Click
the PageWizard
tool on the Publisher toolbar
and select Coupon from the
pop-up menu. *Chapter 14.*

Draw a box on the
back panel—it's
okay that you're
doing this within an
existing text frame.

Choose a
style for the
coupon; in
this case I
think Basic
will work
well. Then
choose Next, and on the following
PageWizard windows tell the PageWizard the
following: The coupon will not be mailed
back; you do not want check boxes for credit
card selections; you do not need an expiration date; and you want a solid border.

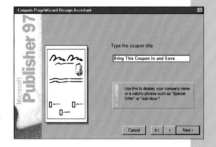

When you
get to the
PageWizard
window that
asks for a title
for the
coupon,
enter your text. Then choose Next
and click Create It.

Use F9 to
zoom in on
the coupon
and replace
the sample
text with your own words.

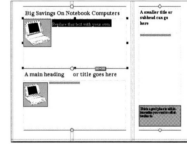

Move to the
first page and
click on the
text frames
so you can
begin replac-
ing the sam-
ple text with the text you want in your
brochure. *Chapter 2.*

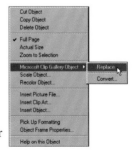

Let's replace one of
the clip art graphics
with something else
(there are two pic-
tures of the same
thing, which is rather
boring). Right-click
on the picture frame and choose Microsoft
Clip Gallery Object, Replace. *Chapter 6.*

20

Choose a new clip art picture. (I chose the calendar page to reinforce the idea that this sale ends when the month

ends.) Choose Insert to place the picture in your brochure, replacing the previous clip art.

21

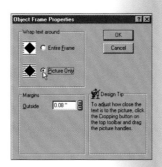

To make the text wrap more professionally around the graphic, right-click on the picture frame and choose Object Frame Properties from the menu. Choose Picture Only as the text wrap option. *Chapter 6.*

22

Hold down the Alt key and use the arrow keys to nudge the picture down and over a bit. *Chapter 12.*

23

Click the graphic in the lower panel to select it, and move it to the center of the panel. Then enlarge it by dragging a corner handle. Hold down both the Shift key (to keep the proportions) and the Ctrl key (to keep the center positioned in the same place) while you drag the handle. *Chapter 6.*

24

Let's replace the heading over this graphic with a fancy element from the Design Gallery. Select the frame and hold down the Ctrl key while you press Del. The frame and its contents disappears.

25

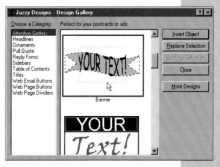

Click the Design Gallery tool on the Publisher toolbar. Choose More Designs, then choose the Jazzy Designs Gallery. Select the banner shown here. *Chapter 14.*

26

Choose Insert Object. The design is placed in the publication and you can move it to its proper position. Use the sizing handles to make it the right size. Since this is WordArt, double-click on it to edit the text. *Chapter 15.*

27

Continue to change the sample text to words and phrases of your own until your brochure is finished. Then run the Spell Checker. *Chapter 11.*

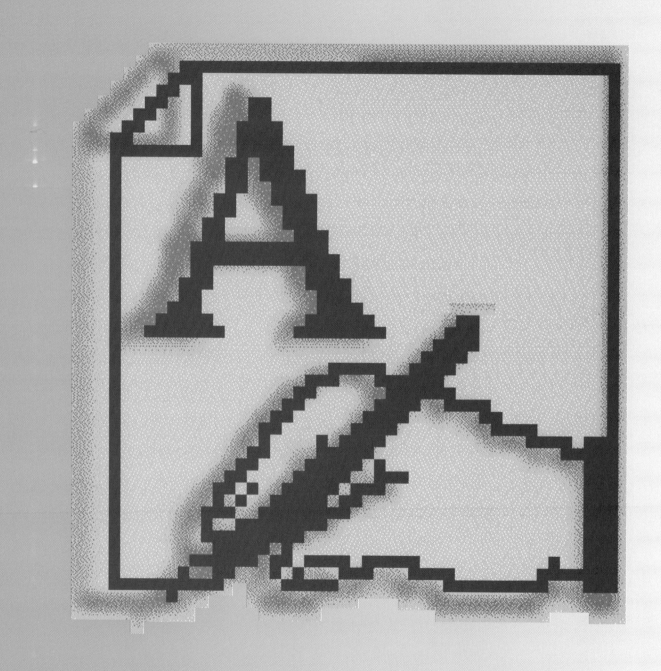

CHAPTER 15

Creating Shapes in Your Publication

Publisher provides shape templates that you can use as special elements in a variety of ways. Sometimes a shape can help send a message; sometimes it just adds zest. Many times, a shape is just the touch you need as a background for text, turning a couple of words into a snappy attention getter.

One of the most creative uses of shapes is to put the text itself into a shape. WordArt, a program built into Publisher, lets you twist and turn text into any number of shapes.

In this chapter you'll learn about shapes and how to insert them into your publication.

How to Use Standard Shapes

Publisher provides a two standard shapes that are frequently useful for adding punch to your publication: the box and the oval. The nice thing about those shapes is that they needn't be standard at all, since you have the opportunity to stretch and bend them to your own taste.

In addition, you can color them and dress them up to make them original and effective.

▶ **1** To use a standard shape in your publication, click on it on the Publisher toolbar.

6 To place text on a shape, create a text frame on the shape and enter the text. Then use Ctrl+T to make the text frame transparent.

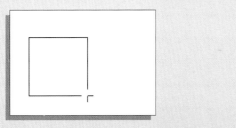

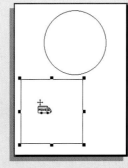

2 To control the placement and shape, place your pointer on the page where you want the shape to appear, then drag the mouse until the shape is the size you need. You can drag the box tool to create a square, a horizontal rectangle, or a vertical rectangle. The oval tool lets you vary the shape in an infinite number of ways, or you can have a perfect circle (hold down the Shift key while you're creating the circle to keep it perfectly round).

3 For single-click placement of the shape, click on the page in the location where you want the shape. Then, if needed, you can move the shape, or adjust it by using the handles.

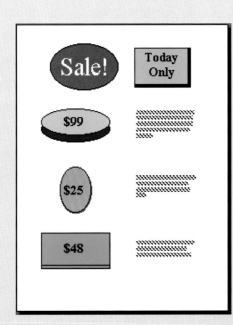

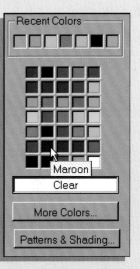

4 To color the shape, make sure it's selected, then choose the Object Color button on the Format toolbar. To add a pattern in addition to color, choose Patterns and Shading after you click the Object Color button, then select Patterns. Choose the pattern design that suits you. To add a gradient, choose Gradients. Then choose a gradient design that matches the look you're trying to achieve. See Chapter 9 for more information on patterns and gradients.

5 You can create a customized shadow for the shape by creating another shape or copying the first one by right-clicking on the shape and choosing the Copy choice from the menu that displays. Then drag one on top of the other, offsetting it just a bit. Color one, then use the Bring To Front and Send To Back buttons on the Standard toolbar to access the other one. Use a contrasting color to create the shadow effect.

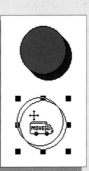

How to Use Custom Shapes

If the standard oval, circle, square, and rectangle don't provide enough pizazz for you, Publisher offers a wide variety of other shapes, called custom shapes. These are frequently useful for calling attention to a page, a particular section of text, or just for dressing up your publication.

▶ **1** To use a custom shape, click the Custom Shapes tool on the Publisher toolbar.

6 As with the standard shapes, you can place text on a custom shape by creating a text frame and making it transparent (press Ctrl+T).

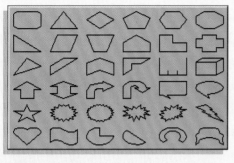

 The custom shapes are displayed so you can choose the one that suits your purpose.

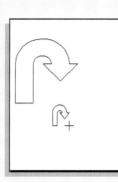

3 Click the custom shape you want to use and then create it by clicking on the page (which creates a large image that you can resize), or by dragging the mouse to control the size yourself.

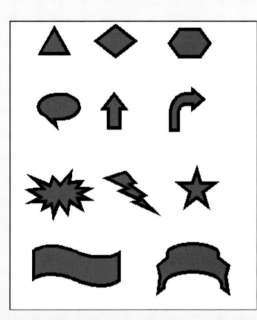

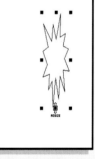

4 Some of the custom shapes can be twisted and reshaped, creating interesting and attention-grabbing patterns. Use the handles to drag the edges and change the shape.

5 You can flip or rotate a custom shape to change its aspect, its personality, or its use. Hold down the Alt key while you drag a handle in the appropriate direction.

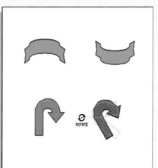

How to Use WordArt

WordArt is a feature that lets you use text as graphics. You can twist and turn words so that they assume a variety of shapes. It's useful for short phrases, jaunty headlines, and attention-getting words. Once you've entered your text, you can create all sorts of effects with the words.

The important thing to remember about WordArt is that it tends to look "busy" and shouldn't be overdone. This is a funky effect and you don't want to use WordArt when passing along somber, serious information.

▶ **1** To create a WordArt object, click the WordArt tool on the Publisher toolbar.

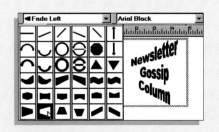

6 The text you entered takes the shape you choose. Click anywhere on the Publisher window outside the WordArt frame to see your creation.

5 Choose a font from the font box, then click the shape box and choose one that fits your needs (or the mood you're trying to establish).

The WordArt text box appears, ready to accept your own text in place of "Your Text Here." Enter the text you want to use. Press Enter when you want to begin a new line.

Choose Update Display to transfer your text into the WordArt frame, then click the X (the Close button) in the upper-right corner to close the text box. Your text is in the WordArt frame and the WordArt Format toolbar is on your Publisher Window.

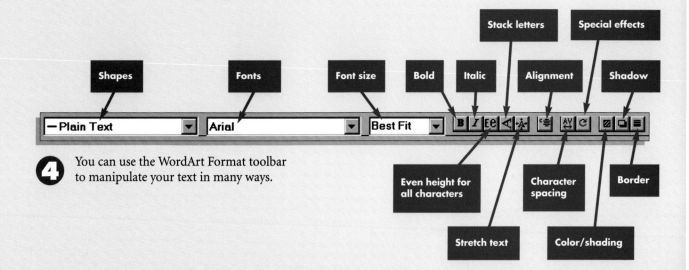

You can use the WordArt Format toolbar to manipulate your text in many ways.

How to Use WordArt (Continued)

Once the WordArt frame is complete, there are plenty of features you can try to make it more interesting, more dynamic, or just more fun.

It's important to remember that even though you're looking at text in the WordArt frame, to Publisher this is a graphic. You can treat it as a graphic frame, including wrapping text around it.

▶ **7** To format and manipulate a WordArt frame, double-click it. The Enter Your Text Here box appears, and if you're not changing the text you can close it. The WordArt Format toolbar remains available for you to work on the frame. A hash-mark border around the frame indicates that the WordArt is in edit mode.

12 You can also manipulate the entire WordArt frame. Click once on it (instead of double-clicking to get to the WordArt graphic inside the frame), then use the formatting tools the way you do with any other graphic frame. For example, you can use the Rotate button or the commands on the Arrange menu to rotate the frame (instead of rotating the text inside the frame as explained above).

Click the Special Effects button on the WordArt Format toolbar. You can rotate the text in small increments by clicking the arrows in the Rotation box (smaller numbers rotate the text clockwise, larger numbers rotate it counter-clockwise). The arrows in the Slider box loosen and tighten the basic shape of the text.

Click the Character Spacing button on the WordArt Format toolbar to change the spacing between characters in the WordArt frame. Sometimes tightening the spacing makes the frame more attractive, and other times (especially with certain shapes) loosening the spacing makes the text easier to read.

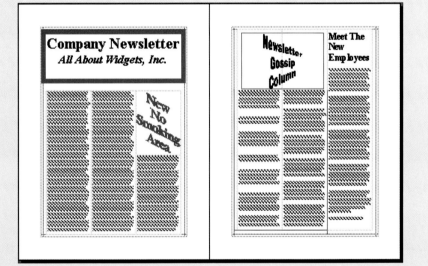

The Equal Height button makes all characters, whether they are uppercase or lowercase, the same height. This can make the WordArt frame more interesting, more artistic, or just funkier.

The Shadow button offers a number of interesting shadow effects to choose from. You can also pick a color for the shadow.

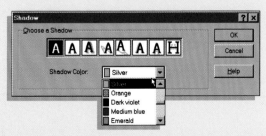

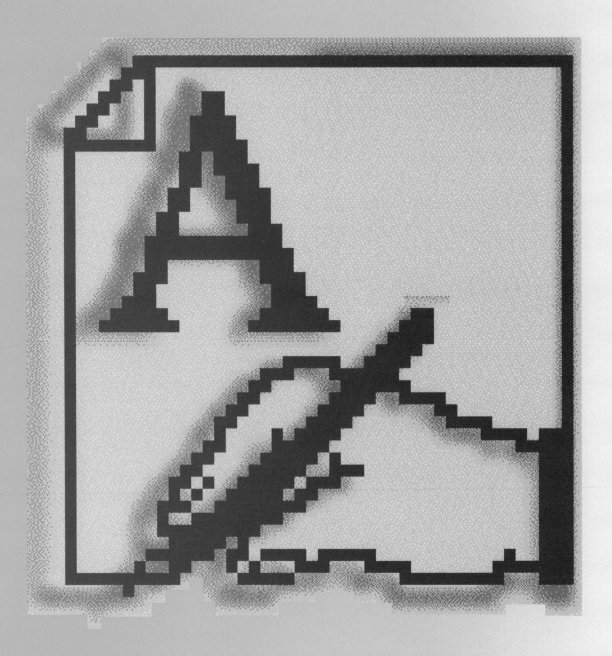

CHAPTER 16

Creating and Editing Tables

There are any number of occasions when a table becomes the most appropriate way to put information in your publication. Tables are especially handy for information that has to kept in columns. An index or table of contents for your publication is easier to create, edit, and read if you use a table. Any sort of multicolumn list you have to present is probably going to be easier to deal with if you use the table format.

In this chapter you'll learn how to create a table and how to enter data into it. You'll also learn about the different formats you can have for tables, using some of the preconfigured formats in Publisher. Each formatting change you make alters the overall appearance of a table, so you can match the style of your publication when you use tables.

How to Create and Format a Table

Publisher provides a number of features for tables, making it easy to use this format for presenting information.

As you begin the process of creating a table, you should remember that its format and appearance should match the information you're planning to put into the table. If you have to present lots of numbers, format the table to make sure that individual rows or columns are easy to read and follow. You may want to make sure there are lines or borders around columns, rows, or both. If the information is simple, short text that is clearly presented in columns or rows, you can dress up your table a bit without worrying about the readability.

▶ **1** To begin creating a table, click the Table tool on the Publisher toolbar.

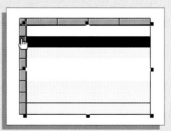

6 Click the column or row selector (the gray box at the top or side of the column or row) to select that column or row. You can then use formatting tools (background color, text attributes, and so forth) that affect only that column or row.

TIP SHEET

▶ **On the Table menu, choose AutoFormat to see the choices for table formats (the same choices that were presented when you began creating the table). If you wish, you can pick a different one. Sometimes, after you've finished entering data, a different format seems to work better.**

▶ **If you drag the handles to resize the table, all the columns or rows (depending on the handle you're dragging) change size and keep their proportionate sizes if you've changed the width of any column or row.**

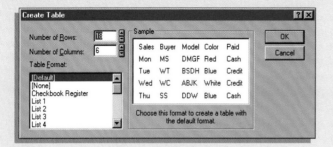

2 Click the page on which you want to place the table. The Create Table dialog box appears.

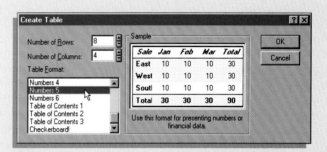

3 Specify the number of rows and number of columns you want in your table by entering the number or using the arrows. Then scroll through the Table Format list to find a format that best presents your information. Click OK.

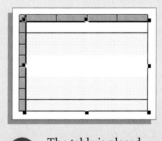

4 The table is placed on your page.

5 Widen or narrow a column or row by placing your pointer on the line between the column or row selector (the gray rectangles on the edge of the table are selectors) until the pointer changes to an Adjust pointer. Then drag the line in the appropriate direction.

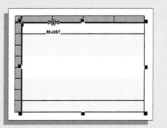

How to Change the Structure and Appearance of a Table

As you begin working with a table, you may find that there's additional information you want to present that requires additional columns. Perhaps the printed copy of your publication is hard to read and you want to delineate the information more clearly.

In this section you'll learn about several formatting changes you can make to solve any problems you have with tables.

► **1** To insert or delete columns or rows, select the table, then choose Table from the menu bar. Use the appropriate command to accomplish the task.

► The upper-left gray selector is the selector for the entire table.

► To change the alignment of the text in a column, click the column selector, then click the appropriate alignment book on the Format toolbar.

► When you choose Insert a Column or Row, a dialog box appears asking whether you want the new column or row before or after the place where your pointer is.

► To add some flair to your page, rotate the table by holding down the Alt key and moving the pointer to a corner handle so it changes to a Rotate pointer. Then drag the handle to the position you want.

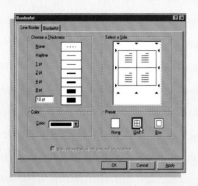

2 To add or change a border, click the border button on the Format toolbar and select a thickness. Select Grid to apply the border to every line in the table, or select Box to border only the outside edges. Click OK.

3 To choose text formatting for a column or row, click the selector to highlight it. Then choose Format, Character from the menu bar. Choose the font, font size, color, style, and effects as needed.

This Month's Results

Name	#	Amount	Team

4 To change the background color of a row or column, click its selector and then click the Object Color tool and select a color. If you don't select a specific row or column, the color is applied to the entire table.

5 To change the margins for cells so you can control how close to the edge of the cell the text is, use the selectors to select the entire table, a row or column, or just drag the mouse over certain cells. Then choose Format, Table Cell Properties from the menu bar.

How to Enter Data in a Table

Of course, the whole purpose of designing and formatting a table is to present information. Most of the time, the data you enter is text, and frequently you enter numbers. But you can also place graphics in a table.

The trick is to avoid making the table too busy, too complicated, or too crowded. Remember that the point of using a table is to make it easier to read the information.

Enter text the same way you enter text in a text frame.

1 To enter text, click on the cell in which you want to begin. You can format the text in the cell in the same manner that you can format text in a text frame. For more detailed information on entering text and formatting it, see Chapters 2 and 3.

6 If all the cells in a row or a column will receive the same text, enter the text for the first cell. Then use the row or column selector to select the row or column. Choose Table, Fill Right (if you've selected a row) or Fill Down (if you've selected a column).

TIP SHEET

▸ **To fine-tune bulleted and numbered lists, use the Indents and Lists dialog box, which you can reach by choosing Format, Indents and Lists, from the menu bar.**

▸ **If you're creating a table that has totals for a particular column in the last row, merge all the cells in the last row except for the column that has the totals. Use the merged cell to title the last row "Totals."**

To move to the next cell, press Tab (press Shift+Tab to move back to the previous cell). Of course, having the Tab key used to move between cells presents a small problem—how do you insert a tab in text? It's simple, just hold down the Ctrl key while you press the Tab key. To set or change the indents for tabs, click on the ruler.

Enter text the same way you enter text in a text frame.

Payroll Preparation for Managers

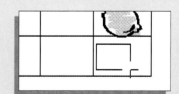

You can use bulleted and numbered lists in a table. Most of the time, you'll find that if these features are needed, they're needed for an entire column. Click the column selector, then use the Bulleted or Numbered List tool on the Format toolbar. (You can also select a single cell and perform the same action.)

To add a graphic to your table, click the Picture tool on the Publisher toolbar. Drag your mouse in the cell to create the frame. Then right-click in the frame and choose Insert Clip Art. Pick the graphic you need.

 To spread text across multiple cells (for example, in the top row when you want the row to be a title for the table), select the cells by dragging your mouse across them. Then choose Table, Merge Cells to create one large cell out of the selected individual cells.

TRY IT!

Now you're ready to try producing another publication using even more Publisher elements. Let's pretend that you've just been named the vice president of your company's in-house publishing unit. You're in charge of "interesting memos." That means you have to create publications that will be distributed to other employees. Since they hate getting corporate memos (because it's almost always about attending a meeting or filling out a report), you have to be creative enough to make them want to read the publications that come from you.

For this exercise, you'll send a mini-newsletter to all employees. As you go through the steps, you'll see references to chapters in italics, which means you can re-read those chapters to get detailed information about the processes you're using.

Start with a blank page. The first element you're going to place on it is an attention getter.
Click the Design Gallery tool on the Publisher toolbar to get started. The Design Gallery window opens. *Chapter 14.*

Choose More Designs and select the Jazzy Designs Gallery.

Scroll through the Attention Getters designs and find the Star. Select it and choose Insert Object.

The design element is placed on the page. Move it to the top of the page. Then use the sizing handles to make it larger.

Double-click on the frame to open the WordArt text editor. Change the text to match the message you want to present in your publication. Choose Update Display to move the new text into the WordArt frame. *Chapter 15.*

Click the Text tool and put a text frame under the headline. *Chapter 2.*

Press F9 to zoom in and enter text as shown.

Format the text, making it larger, bold, and centered in the frame. Use the buttons on the Format toolbar. *Chapter 3.*

Create another text frame below the one you just finished. You'll use this frame to enter a list of items.

Continue to next page ▶

TRY IT!

Continue below

10 Click the Bulleted or Numbered List button on the Format tool-bar and select a bullet style as shown here. *Chapter 11.*

11 Zoom in and enter text as shown. Note that each time you press Enter, a new bullet appears automatically.

- Government reports, including OSHA, are now the responsibility of the Administrative Group. The R&D group will no longer handle these chores.
- Requests for vacation, personal days and other pre-planned time off will be delivered to Human Resources instead of Payroll.
- There is a new form for department heads for overtime approvals. This form is delivered to Human Resources instead of Payroll.
- The IS Help Desk will no longer respond to requests from users to install software. All software that is permitted is installed from the servers. Please do not bring software disks into the building.

12 Select the text by dragging your mouse over it. Then change the font to 12 points. Notice that the text rewraps. *Chapter 3.*

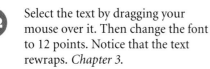

- Government reports, including OSHA, are now the responsibility of the Administrative Group. The R&D group will no longer handle these chores.
- Requests for vacation, personal days and other pre-planned time off will be delivered to Human Resources instead of Payroll.
- There is a new form for department heads for overtime approvals. This form is delivered to Human Resources instead of Payroll.
- The IS Help Desk will no longer respond to requests from users to install software. All software that is permitted is installed from the servers. Please do not bring software disks into the building.

13 Press Enter after the last line of text, then click the Bulleted or Numbered List button on the Format toolbar and choose None to turn off bullets.

14 Press Enter again to create a blank line, then enter regular text as seen here.

form is delivered to Human Resources instead of Payroll.
- The IS Help Desk will no longer respond to requests from users to install software. All software that is permitted is installed from the servers. Please do not bring software disks into the building.

Any department heads that need additional information about implementing the new assignments and procedures should call Mrs. Goldman at Ext. 431. The effective date for these rules changes is March 1st. However, you can begin implementation immediately.

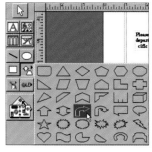

15 Zoom out to see the entire page. Click the Custom Shapes tool on the Publisher toolbar and select the curved arrow. *Chapter 15.*

16

Click on the
text frame
you were just
working on
to place the
arrow in it.

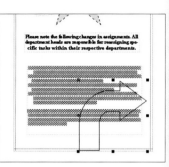

17

Use the resiz-
ing handles
to make the
arrow
smaller. Then
move the arrow to the
lower right corner of
the text frame.

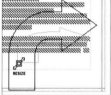

18

Click the Object
Color tool on the
Format toolbar
and choose a color
for the arrow.
Chapter 15.

19

Use the Flip
Horizontal
button on the
Graphics
toolbar
point the
arrow toward the text. Then hold down
the Alt key and use the sizing handles
to rotate the arrow slightly. *Chapter 15.*

20

You now have an
interesting, graph-
ical format for
passing along
some rather mun-
dane information.

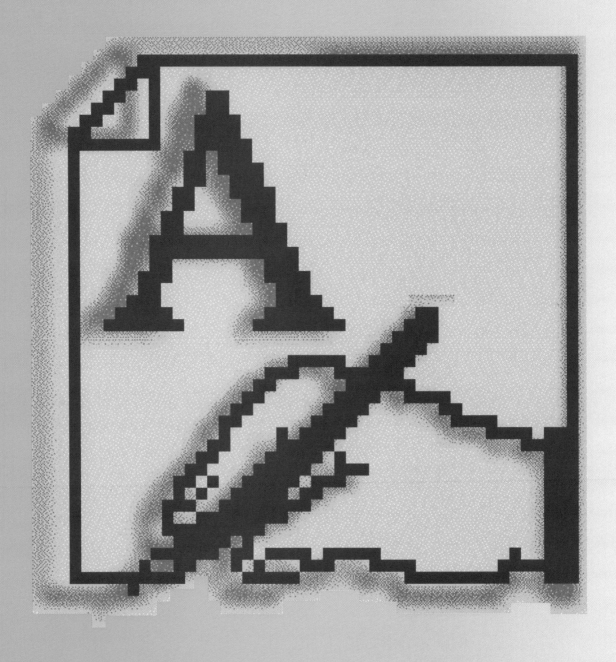

CHAPTER 17

Working with OLE Objects

Sometimes you need a special element that would make your publication absolutely perfect, but you find that Publisher cannot produce such an element. No problem. You can create the element in software that is designed to do what you need and then use Windows's OLE capabilities to bring it into your publication. In this chapter you'll learn about inserting sound, animated video clips, and charts into your publication.

OLE means Object Linking and Embedding. It's one of those terms that computer weenies use all the time, and it may sound complicated, but it isn't. It means there's an object in a document in one Windows program that is linked to or embedded from a document in another Windows program.

If the object is linked, it appears in your publication but it is stored outside of your publication. Your publication holds the link (it's like an address) and when you want to view or print your publication Publisher reads the address, fetches the object, and provides it. If the original object is changed, the next time you link to it you see the changes (or hear them, if it's a sound).

If the object is embedded, it is moved into your publication after it's created and becomes a part of your publication, just like the artwork or text you create while you work in Publisher.

Inserting Embedded Sound Objects

More and more, people are adding sound capabilities to their computers. If you want to use your publication as a media event, showing it to an audience via a computer, you can use sound to jazz up your production. There's no way (yet) to provide sound effects when you print and distribute your publication.

If your computer isn't equipped for sound, you probably will get an error message when you attempt to use a program that creates sound objects.

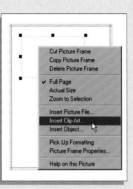

▶**1** The easiest way to insert a sound object is to use the Sounds tab on the Clip Art dialog box. To get there, create a picture frame on the page, then right-click on the frame and choose Insert Clip Art.

5 If you want an amusement break, choose Play and listen to your selection. The player controls appear and as the selection plays the slider moves to the right. You can pause, restart, and stop the music with the buttons on the control panel. Choose Stop Playing in the dialog box to stop the music and quit the control window.

2 If this is the first time you've used a sound, there won't be anything in the Sounds tab. To add sounds, choose Import Clips, which lets you bring sound files into your Clip Gallery. Once the sounds are there, they'll be available to you in the future. These are embedded objects.

3 The Add Sounds to Clip Gallery dialog box opens and is probably displaying the folder where Publisher is kept. Use the tools on this window's toolbar to move through your computer's folders. Find the folder where Windows 95 is installed (or Windows NT 4, if that's what you're using). Then find a folder named Media.

4 When you double-click on the Media folder, all the sound files contained in it are displayed. Pick the one you want by double-clicking on it. The Clip Properties dialog box appears with your selection in it. Publisher wants information about the sound file before placing it in the Clip Gallery. You can add Keywords to search on, and you have to choose a category (or create a new one). On my system, I created a new category called Sounds.

Inserting Embedded Sound Objects (Continued)

Now that you've chosen a sound file (by the way, the jargon for this is "sound bite" or "sound clip," which comes from the broadcasting industry), you can add it to your Clip Gallery and place it in your publications.

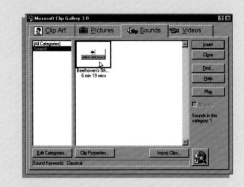

▶ ⑥ After you've picked a category, choose OK on the Clip Properties dialog box to put this sound clip into the Gallery. Notice that the length of the sound clip is noted below its icon.

Select the sound clip and choose Insert (or double-click on the sound clip) to bring it into your publication. Your picture frame now contains this sound clip.

JAN	FEB	MAR	APR	MAY
$2,000	$500	$1,000	♫ ♫	$2,050
$2,500	$1,500	$900	♫ ♫	$2,560
$1,000	$845	$1,500	$1,800	$1,400
$2,353	$1,353	$2,000	$2,000	$2,300
$1,009	$1,200	$1,300	$1,000	$1,110
$3,000	$2,000	$3,000	$1,700	$3,040
$2,900	$1,900	$1,700	$1,300	$2,500

8 Continue to create elements for the page. The sound frame is just another element and you can make it as large or as small as you wish.

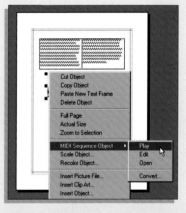

9 To play the sound clip, right-click on its frame and choose it from the menu (the object on the menu matches the type of sound clip you inserted, which might be a MIDI sound or a Wave sound), then choose Play from the submenu. MIDI and Wave sounds are supplied with your Windows 95 operating system and they are usually used to create the sound effects you hear when you open Windows 95, or when you make an error. Read the Windows 95 Help files for advanced information about sound files.

10 Use the control buttons to stop and play the sound clip.

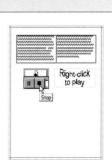

Inserting Linked Sound Objects

It's not necessary to bring a sound clip into your Clip Gallery; you can place a link to an existing sound file into your publication. Of course, if you send the publication to another user via e-mail, that user must have the same file in the same folder in order to make the link work.

If you're using sound files provided by your operating system (Windows 95 or Windows NT 4) and the recipient of your publication has the same operating system (and has installed the sound files in the same folder) there won't be a problem.

1 To place a linked OLE object in your publication, click the OLE tool on the Publisher toolbar. A menu appears that lists all OLE objects you've chosen during the time you've used Publisher (usually you'll see Microsoft Clip Gallery and perhaps Microsoft Drawing, depending on what you've created). If there's no sound object listed, choose More to see the Insert Object dialog box.

Since you're going to link a file, choose Create from File. The dialog box changes to allow you to enter the path and file name (or choose Browse to find a file). Select Link to link the file instead of embedding it. Click OK.

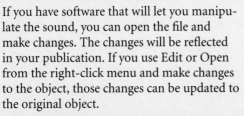

The object is placed in a picture frame in your publication. Go ahead and continue to create text and graphic frames in your publication.

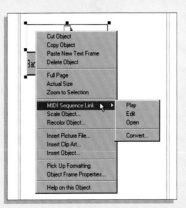

To play your sound clip, right-click on its frame. Notice that the menu item includes the word Link. Choose Play from the submenu.

If you have software that will let you manipulate the sound, you can open the file and make changes. The changes will be reflected in your publication. If you use Edit or Open from the right-click menu and make changes to the object, those changes can be updated to the original object.

How to Work with Charts and Graphs from Other Applications

If you need to present information in a manner that Publisher doesn't provide, you can use another software program to create the information and bring it into your publication.

A common situation is the need for a spreadsheet, or a graph from a spreadsheet. Or perhaps you own an application that produces special types of documents (for instance, MS PowerPoint or a program that captures photographs) and you want to bring an element from that software into your publication.

1 To create a new object in another software application in order to bring it into your publication, click the OLE tool and choose More to display the Insert Object dialog box. Make sure Create New is selected, then scroll to the type of object you want to create and click OK.

6 If you choose Display as Icon in the Insert Object dialog box, instead of seeing the object on your page you see an icon representing it. Double-click the icon to open the creating application in order to view or manipulate the object.

2 The tools from the creating application are made available to you right in your Publisher window. In fact, some of the toolbars change to those of the creating application, even though you haven't left Publisher.

3 Create the object, using these tools. Remember that the menu bar and tools belong to the creating application (even though the title bar on your window says you're working in Publisher), so you can get help and have access to features.

4 When you are finished creating the object, click anywhere on the Publisher window, outside the page. The object is inserted on your page, and the Publisher menu bar and toolbars return.

5 If you want to use an existing object from another software application (a file you already created and saved in that application), when you are making selections in the Insert Object dialog box, choose Create from File. Then enter the file name or Browse to find it.

How to Insert Video Clips

Video clips (mini motion pictures) can be inserted, embedded, or linked similar to the way sound clips added. That is, you can bring animated video clips into your Publisher Clip Gallery so they can be used in future publications, or you can embed or link them from their source applications.

Video brings a real flair to your publication, as long as the publication is shown via computer. You can't, of course, take advantage of motion pictures in a printed document.

▶ **1** To insert a video clip into your publication and also put it into your clip gallery so you can use it again, put a picture frame on the page. Right-click in the frame and choose Insert Clip Art. When the Clip Gallery opens, move to the Videos tab.

TIP SHEET

▶ As with sound clips, linking video instead of embedding it is a way to save disk space. Video files are quite large.

▶ Yet another shortcut the Insert Object dialog box is the right-click menu in Publisher, which contains Insert Object as a menu item.

Choose Import Clips to bring up the Add Videos to Clip Gallery dialog box. Use the toolbar to move around your system to find the folder that has video clips. When you find the clip you want, double-click it.

Fill in the information about this clip and choose OK to put it into the Clip Gallery. Select it and choose Insert to place it in your publication. Then when you want to watch it, right-click on it and select Video Clip Object, Play.

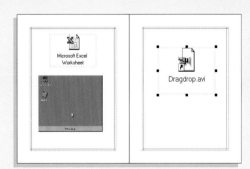

 To link a video, follow step 4, but select Link. You may also want to select Display as Icon. Choose OK to place the linked file in your publication.

To embed a video, click the OLE tool and choose More. In the Insert Object dialog box choose Create from File, then enter the path and file name for the video. Choose OK to place the video into your publication.

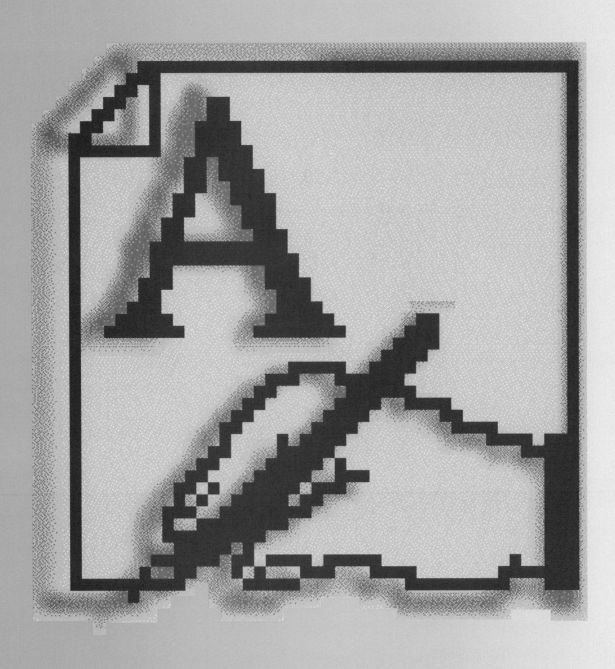

CHAPTER 18

Creating Custom-Sized Posters and Banners

Even though your printer will handle only a limited size of paper, Publisher allows you to design and produce larger publications. Oversized posters and large banners can be designed and produced in-house using the special features for these items that are built into Publisher.

These are a lot of fun to design and create. This is not your average corporate production, where you have to find a creative way to display the revenue stream or a list of employee phone numbers. This is for special occasions—for example, a poster announcing an important event or a banner you want to hang across a room when the event takes place.

How to Create a Banner or Poster

This is one area where you don't want to re-invent a wheel that Publisher has already invented. Since the real complications and the real work are in the printing, make the design process as easy as possible. Use Publisher's PageWizard to design and create your publication.

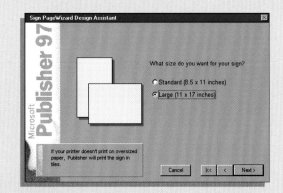

▶ **1** If you've just started Publisher, you'll see the PageWizard in the opening window. But if you're already working in Publisher you have to bring it up manually. To do that, choose File, Create New Publication.

5 To create an oversized poster, after step 1 choose Sign as the publication, then choose Other as the Type. Follow the same process of answering questions and making decisions. When you're asked about size, choose Large. Create your text and let Publisher do the rest.

TIP SHEET

▶ When you're designing a banner, the longer you make it, the more text you can fit in it.

▶ If you chose to add graphics to your banner or poster, and the text seems too small, you can delete the graphic frame and enlarge the text.

▶ Banners and oversized posters are publications just like any other publication, so you can select the text frame and manipulate it, change the font, change the attributes, and so on.

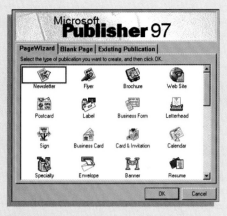

2 The PageWizard window opens so you can use it to create a new publication. If you want to create a banner, click on Banner and then click OK.

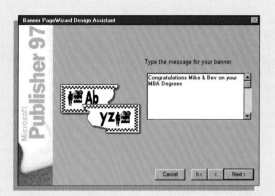

3 The PageWizard asks about the style of banner you want (for instance, classic, modern, or wild), and lets you decide on height and length, and whether or not you want graphics. Answer according to your taste and the purpose of your banner, choosing Next to move on after each answer. Then enter the message for the banner and choose Next. The PageWizard tells you to relax while it creates the banner. Click Create It to start that process.

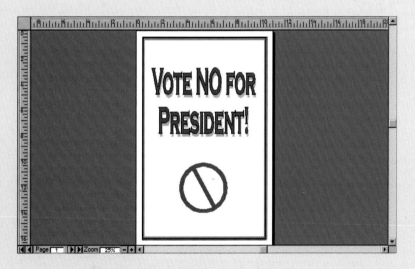

4 Your banner appears on your Publisher window.

How to Print Banners and Posters

This is where the complications arrive. Your printer doesn't handle paper that is eight feet in length. Your commercial print shop probably faces the same problem. Get ready to cut and paste.

If you've ever seen a fancy tiled wall, with individual tiles providing parts of a pattern that is one large display when all the tiles are put together, you can visualize what you're going to do in order to print your banner. In fact, this printing process is called "tile printing" in Publisher.

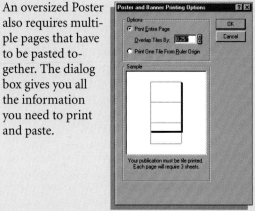

▶ **1** With the banner or poster in the Publisher window, choose File, Print from the menu bar (or press Ctrl+P).

6 An oversized Poster also requires multiple pages that have to be pasted together. The dialog box gives you all the information you need to print and paste.

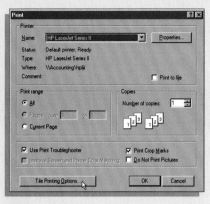

2 When the Print dialog box appears, skip the normal selection options. Instead, choose Tile Printing Options.

3 The Poster and Banner Printing Options dialog box sets up the print job for your oversized publication. It tells you the number of pages that have to be printed in order to print the complete publication. And it tells you the size of the overlap it's allowing (which is your guide to cutting and/or pasting). You can choose OK to print all the pages. You are returned to the Print dialog box, where you should click OK to begin the printing.

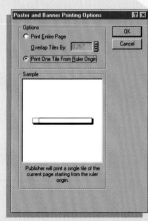

Crop marks

5 Select Print One Tile From Ruler Origin to print one page of the banner. The page that prints is the part of the banner that is closest to the rulers on the Publisher window (see the Tip Sheet on this page for instructions about changing the ruler origin). The Sample section of the dialog box indicates the page that will print.

4 When the pages are printed, they have crop marks as guidelines so you can paste them together properly.

CHAPTER 19

Using the Design Checker

It's not easy being perfect all by yourself. A pair of watchful eyes, looking over your shoulder, can help you do everything exactly the way it's supposed to be done. Publisher has a watchdog, a second pair of eyes, called the Design Checker, that can check your publication. Like the junior high school English teacher of your nightmares, nothing gets by the Design Checker.

In this chapter you'll learn how to put the Design Checker to work on a publication, and you'll learn how to configure and set up the Design Checker for certain tasks. That way, you can run a fast test of your publication against those tasks.

Letting Design Checker Check Everything

The way to ensure perfection is to let the Design Checker loose on your publication. It is a compulsive, obsessive, detail-oriented, nagging overseer. It shows no mercy, takes no prisoners. What more could you ask for as you search for perfection?

▶ **1** To let Publisher's Design Checker go over your publication with an eagle eye, open the publication. Then choose Tools, Design Checker from the menu bar.

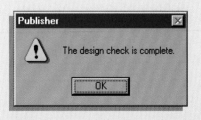

6 Some of the other problems that the Design Checker will point out are the presence of more than three fonts or three colors at one time (tacky, tacky), two spaces after a period at the end of a sentence (one space is the publishing standard), or a frame's overlap into an area of the page that your printer can't print on. When you've corrected the problems (or ignored them), the Design Checker announces that its work is done.

2 The Design Checker dialog box has default settings for checking all the pages, including background pages. There's usually no reason to change that, so click OK to start the process.

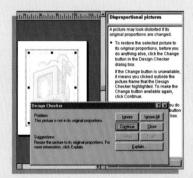

3 The Design Checker stops at every element where it finds a problem. You may not share that feeling, and you may be perfectly happy with an element that the Design Checker finds problematic.

4 Choose Ignore if you don't want to do anything about the perceived problem. Choose Ignore All if you don't want the Design Checker to tell you about this particular problem again if it finds another example. Choose Explain to see an explanation of the problem, along with some ideas for fixing it (you may have to move the Design Checker out of the way to read the whole thing—just point to the title bar and drag it over).

5 If you do want to fix a problem, click on the frame that needs work and do whatever is necessary to correct the problem. Then choose Continue on the Design Checker dialog box.

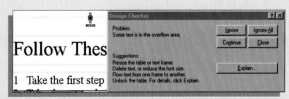

Checking for Specific Problems

Some of the things that the Design Checker calls problematic may be perfectly fine in your opinion. It may not bother you that pictures in your publication aren't proportioned the way they are in the Clip Art Gallery. Perhaps you only stretched them, or shrunk them a bit at the sides to make them fit your page and you're sure nobody will notice (well, nobody but the Design Checker).

You can decide which problems you want the Design Checker to worry about. And sometimes you'll want to check for only one or two problems as an interim check, waiting until you finish to do a full check.

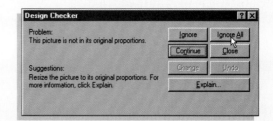

1 The quickest way to stop the Design Checker from telling you about something you don't think is a problem is to click Ignore All the first time the problem arises.

Design Checker

Problem:
This picture is not in its original proportions.

Ignore | Ignore All
Continue | Close
Change | Undo

Suggestions:
Resize the picture to its original proportions. For more information, click Explain.

Explain...

 For out-of-proportion pictures, it might be worthwhile trying the Change button to see if it makes the publication look better. When a graphic problem is found, the graphic is selected by the Design Checker so you can fix it easily. If you click Change and then don't like the result, just click the Undo button.

Design Checker

Check which pages?
○ All
○ Pages
from: 1   to: 26

OK
Cancel
Options...

☑ Check background page(s)

3 The best way to configure the Design Checker to tell you about the things that *you* consider problematic is to choose Options from the Design Checker dialog box that displays when you first invoke it from the menu.

Feeling
a
little
stretched?

Options

○ Check selected features
○ Check all problems

OK
Cancel

☑ Empty frames
☑ Covered objects
☑ Text in overflow area
☑ Objects in nonprinting region
☐ Disproportional pictures
☐ Too many special effects
☑ Spacing between sentences
☐ Too many fonts
☐ Too many colors

4 First, select Check Selected Features (which deselects Check All Problems, the default state of the options). Then go through the list and deselect the problems that don't bother you. Choose OK when your list matches your concerns.

 Don't deselect the serious problems, and don't ignore them when the Design Checker finds them. Get in the habit of fixing them on the spot—you may not remember to go back to fix them later.

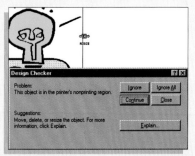

Design Checker

Problem:
This object is in the printer's nonprinting region.

Ignore | Ignore All
Continue | Close

Suggestions:
Move, delete, or resize the object. For more information, click Explain.

Explain...

CHAPTER 20

Printing Your Work

Eventually, when you've created a publication that's a master-piece, you'll want other people to see it. Even if it isn't a mas-terpiece, you probably have no choice about it, since most publications are created for the express purpose of being distributed.

You have some choices about the way your publication is printed, and this chapter covers the options available to you.

How to Set Up Your Printer

Depending upon the printer you're using, there are choices you can make about the way your publication prints. For one thing, you'll want to make sure your printer knows to expect the paper size you've designated for your publication if you used a nonstandard size. You can also change the resolution of text and graphics to print a test copy quickly, and then print the real thing with the proper resolution.

▶**1** To begin setting up the printing process, make sure your publication is loaded in the Publisher window. Then choose File, Print Setup.

6 If you're using a color printer, set the color options. These vary from printer to printer. If you're not sure about the results of your choices, check the documentation that came with the printer.

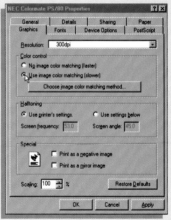

5 *Dithering* is the process of blending basic colors (or tones of gray if you aren't printing to a color printer) to create the colors (or gray shades) you need. If you're using line art for graphics and don't need shades of color or gray, change the Dithering option to Line Art. If you're printing photographs or other similar graphics that don't have clearly defined lines, especially around the edges of images, choose Error Diffusion. If you change the resolution to under 200 dots per inch, change the Dithering to Fine to help clarify the printed images.

TIP SHEET

▶ Remember that you don't need special paper for oversized documents. They print on regular-size paper and you paste the pages together to form the finished publication.

▶ Publisher takes note of the printer that is currently selected when you create a publication. If you change printers, Publisher notices and tells you it is reconfiguring the publication to match the new printer. You will have to check every page of your publication to make sure the changes didn't disturb anything. In fact, it's probably a good idea to run the Design Checker, especially to check for elements that may fall in the non-printing area for the new printer.

2 The Print Setup dialog box appears and you can specify settings for the print job you're about to run.

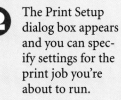

3 Most of the time, there's a limit to the paper sizes a printer will accept. For example, laser printers have special trays for specific sizes and if the correct tray isn't in the printer, you can't use that paper. You can usually specify Manual Feed in that case (which means you have to stand over the printer to feed the paper in).

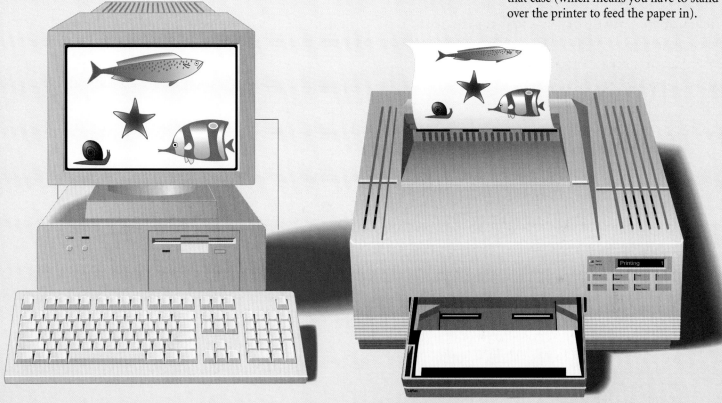

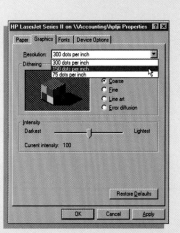

4 Click on Properties to move to the Printer's Properties dialog box. Click the Graphics tab to control the resolution. If you're having a test run to check the placement and overall look of the publication, you can reduce the resolution to make the printing process faster (and use less toner). If you have graphics in your publication, don't reduce the resolution below 150 dots per inch, or you may not be able to make out the graphic's real shape.

How to Print Your Publication

Once everything is set up perfectly, it's time to print your publication. Actually, you can do a test run to your screen by choosing View, Hide Boundaries and Guides. This displays your publication in much the same way that it will print (see the center graphic in this section as an example).

▶ **1** Choose File, Print (or press Ctrl+P) to begin printing your publication.

TIP SHEET

▸ **If your publication is displaying a two-page view, selecting Current Page as a printing option will cause both pages to print.**

▸ **Select Do Not Print Pictures to have the printed copy substitute place holders (gray boxes) for your graphics frames. This is a good way to print a proof copy for someone else to check.**

▸ **If you don't currently have access to the printer, choose Print to File. Later you can send that file to the printer (see the instructions in your operating system Help files). You will be asked for a file name for the print file.**

6 Once you've printed your publication and found that everything worked perfectly, you can avoid using the Print dialog box in the future. Just click the Print tool on the Standard toolbar to print the entire publication automatically.

The Print dialog box displays and you can change any of the options to suit yourself. For example, you may want to print only the current page (the page that's in the Publisher window) or a range of pages (enter the page numbers as x–y, where x is the first page you want to print and y is the last page in the range).

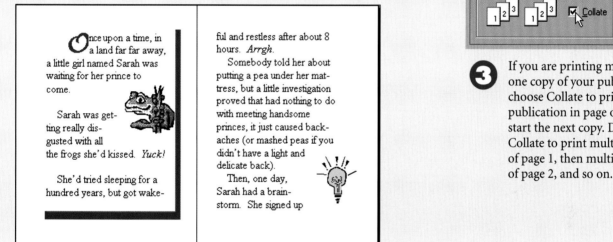

Once upon a time, in a land far far away, a little girl named Sarah was waiting for her prince to come.

Sarah was getting really disgusted with all the frogs she'd kissed. *Yuck!*

She'd tried sleeping for a hundred years, but got wakeful and restless after about 8 hours. *Arrgh*.

Somebody told her about putting a pea under her mattress, but a little investigation proved that had nothing to do with meeting handsome princes, it just caused backaches (or mashed peas if you didn't have a light and delicate back).

Then, one day, Sarah had a brainstorm. She signed up

3 If you are printing more than one copy of your publication, choose Collate to print the publication in page order, then start the next copy. Deselect Collate to print multiple copies of page 1, then multiple copies of page 2, and so on.

4 Unless you deselect the option on the Print dialog box, the Publisher Print Troubleshooter opens as soon as you begin printing.

 If the print job didn't turn out the way you expected, click the arrow next to Troubleshoot Printing Problem. Then select your problem from the list in the Print Troubleshooter. As you move through the Print Troubleshooter, you'll continue to answer questions and make further selections.

Using an Outside Printing Service

Almost all professional printing companies accept disks these days. And there are printing service companies that specialize in printing from customer disks. This is a terrific way to get high resolution, full-color printing for your important publications.

Before you start, contact the printing service and ascertain exactly what they need from you. They may need to set up a specific printer and attach it to your publication, or they may want a generic PostScript file.

When you first installed Publisher you were asked if you wanted to install the Publisher printer drivers. These drivers provide PostScript capabilities, which is what you'll probably need for outside printing. If you didn't install those drivers, go back to the Publisher installation program and do it now.

1 Once the Publisher printer drivers are transferred to your hard drive, you have to add a printer to your system, using those drivers. Open My Computer in your Windows 95 or Windows NT 4 operating system and double-click on Add Printer. Follow the Add Printer Wizard's directions (make it a local printer, don't print a test page, and don't make it the default printer).

5 If you choose Select a Specific Printer, click the double arrow to see a dialog box that displays a list of all the printers installed on your system. Choose the printer you need for this outside service. Choose OK to return to this dialog box, then choose Done.

TIP SHEET

▸ **Once you've selected the printer, Publisher will probably tell you it wants to change the publication to match the printer. Answer Yes, then use the Design Checker once more before continuing.**

▸ **You can pretty much count on the fact that PostScript is PostScript. If you don't have the Publisher driver installed, install any PostScript printer. The codes that are sent to the printer should be the same.**

2 Open the publication you're sending to the printing service. Then choose File, Outside Print Setup.

File	Edit	View	Insert	Format	Tools	Arrange	T
Create New Publication...					Ctrl+N		
Open Existing Publication...					Ctrl+O		
Create Web Site from Current Publication							
Close Publication							
Save					Ctrl+S		
Save As...							
Find File...							
Page Setup...							
Print Setup...							
Print...					Ctrl+P		
Outside Print Setup...							
Print to Outside Printer...							
Print InfoSheet							
Send...							
1 C:\Program Files\Microsoft P...\art1							
2 C:\Program Files\Microsoft P...\art2							
3 C:\Program Files\Microsoft P...\annc1							
4 C:\Program Files\Microsoft P...\poster							
Exit Publisher					Alt+F4		

Outside Print Setup

Step 1: What type of printing do you want from your printing service?

Publisher supports the following types of printing:

○ I've decided not to use a commercial printing service, thanks.

○ Black, white, and shades of gray, on any printer.

● Full color, on a color printer at less than 1200 dpi resolution.

○ Spot color(s) at greater than 1200 dpi resolution.
(Black, white, and gray plus tints of up to two additional colors.)

[Cancel] [<< Back] [>> Next]

3 The Outside Print Setup dialog box displays the choices you have for printing. Select the one that fits your circumstances. Choose Next.

4 Select either the MS Publisher outside printer driver or a specific printer that your printing service prefers. Remember that you have to install this printer before you can finish this process. Choose Done.

Outside Print Setup

Step 2: What printer will you use?

You can use Publisher's outside printer driver that will enable your publication to print on most printing devices.

Your printer is currently set to: MS Publisher Color Printer

● Use Publisher's outside printer driver.

○ Select a specific printer.

[Cancel] [<< Back] [Done]

Using an Outside Printing Service (Continued)

Once the Outside Print Setup is complete, you're ready to turn your publication file into a printer file. In effect, you're going to print your publication to a printer that isn't connected to your computer (or any computer on the network that's acting as a printer server). Instead, you'll print to a file and take the file to the printing service.

Besides your publication file, there's an information file you'll print (either to paper through your own printer, or to a disk file) that will help the outside printing service do the job properly.

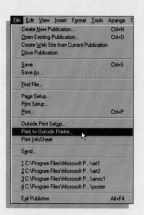

▶ **6**   To begin printing the publication for the outside printer, choose File, Print to Outside Printer from the menu bar.

TIP SHEET

▶ You can print the InfoSheet and Proof at any time, not just after you've printed to the outside service file. Both items are on the File menu.

▶ If your outside printing service can't handle bleeds, just have them print your pages on larger paper. Then the bleed area won't be at the edge of the paper. Of course, you'll have to incur a charge for cutting the paper back to its proper size.

▶ If your publication is set up for spot color, you can print a separation proof for each color. Spot color is the term for adding one or two colors to certain objects in a basically black, white, and gray publication. It's useful for adding color to symbols or attention-getting objects on a page.

Print to Outside Printer

Printer
Name: Linotronic 630   Properties...
Type: Linotronic 630
☑ Print to file

Print range
◉ All 5 pages
○ Pages from: 1 to: 5
○ Current Page

Copies
Number of copies: 1
☑ Collate

☑ Use Print Troubleshooter
☐ Improve Screen and Printer Color Matching
☑ Print Color Separations
☑ Show all print marks
☑ Allow Bleeds

Book Printing Options...   OK   Cancel

7 The Print to Outside Printer dialog box appears and it is configured to print the job to a file (notice the selection of Print to File). Your dialog box may show the MS Publisher printer; mine shows the printer my outside service suggested.

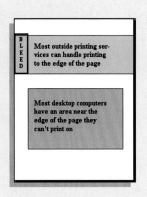

B L E E D — Most outside printing services can handle printing to the edge of the page

Most desktop computers have an area near the edge of the page they can't print on

8 Check with your printing service about bleeds, especially if you're using color backgrounds on any pages. If they cannot handle bleeds be sure to deselect Allow Bleeds on the dialog box.

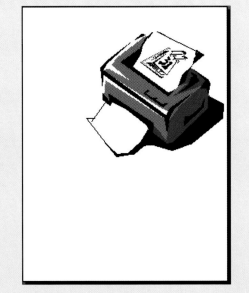

Print To File

File name:
AnnRpt.prn

Folders:
C:\Progr...\Microsoft Publisher
📁 c:\
📁 Program Files
📁 Microsoft Publisher
📁 Backgrnd
📁 Backup
📁 Borders

Save file as type:
Printer Files

Drives:
💾 c:

OK
Cancel
Network...

9 When you've checked the details, choose OK. The Print to file dialog box appears. Enter a file name (Publisher will add the extension .PRN automatically), and choose a folder for it. Click on OK. Copy the file to a disk and deliver it (or upload it to the service's e-mail address).

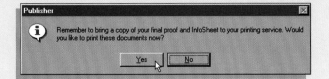

Publisher

ℹ️ Remember to bring a copy of your final proof and InfoSheet to your printing service. Would you like to print these documents now?

Yes   No

10 It's a good idea to send your outside service a proof copy, which is a rendition of the publication they can use as a guideline, and an InfoSheet, which gives them technical information about the file. Publisher offers to print these and you should accept the offer by choosing Yes. Both documents are printed by your regular printer.

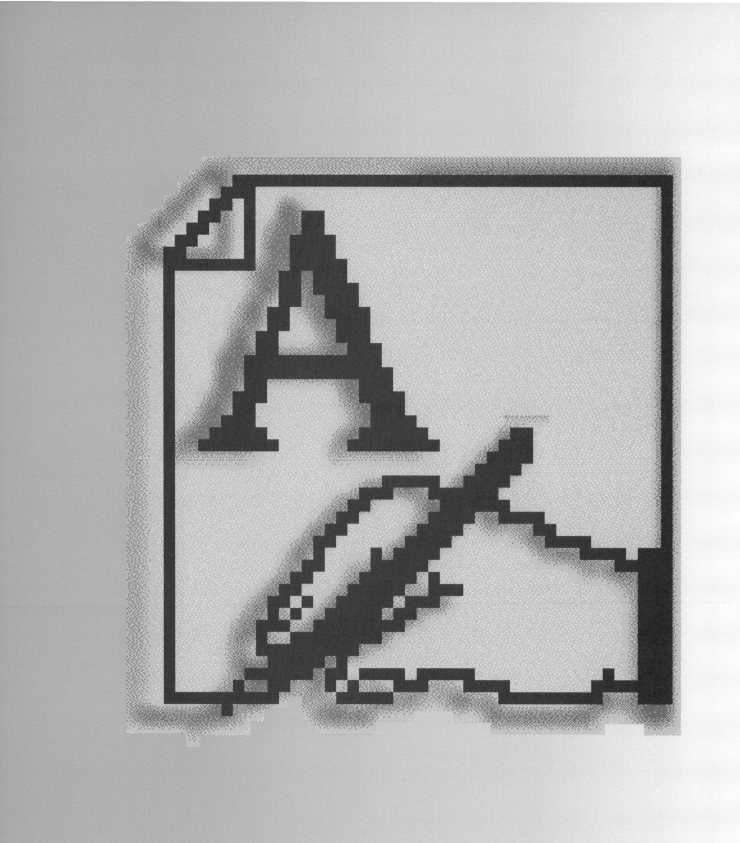

CHAPTER 21

Useful and Fun Publications

In the old days people called on each other by actually visiting in person. The front hall of every home had a small tray or bowl to receive the calling cards of visitors who stopped by. Today, people exchange business cards. Even if you have a formal business card, there are times when a personal card might be more appropriate.

In this chapter we'll look at a few of the publications Publisher has prepared for you so you just have to fill in the details to make use of them. Some of them are business items such as forms and business cards, which you can design to fit your personal needs. Some of them are for your own personal use and enjoyment, including paper airplanes and greeting cards.

Business Forms, Business Cards, Envelopes, and More

Whether you have a business or not, you probably have use for personalized, customized forms, cards, and other printed items used in business.

You can use Publisher's pre-formatted forms to create what you need, or you can disassemble them and rearrange them to suit your own taste. And, of course, you could build your printed forms from scratch.

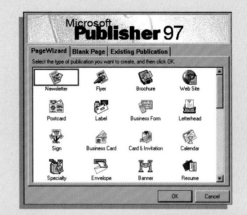

1 To use Publisher's preformatted publications, choose File, Create New Publication from the menu bar. The PageWizard tab of the Publication window opens.

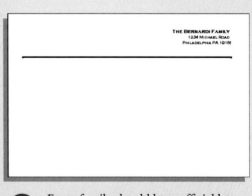

6 Every family should have official letterhead. In fact, it's so easy to produce it, you should probably make letterhead for each individual member of the family in addition to the family version. If it suits your family's status, add a fancy seal or crest.

Choose Business Card to create a business card (or calling card). Or choose Envelope or Letterhead to produce those items for yourself. Try Business Form to see a variety of forms you can use in business or personally (for example, a fax form isn't just used in business). Click OK when you have made a choice.

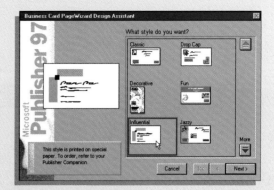

Regardless of your choice of printed item, you'll be asked to choose a style. Pick one that fits your personality, or your mood at the moment. Then choose Next. Depending on the item, you might have to provide other information, such as a name, address, telephone number, or other text.

When your publication is finished, it's displayed in the Publisher window. You can make whatever changes you wish to the elements, text, or colors. For business cards, the publication assumes that an outside printing service will do the printing (and cutting), so cards are printed with multiple images.

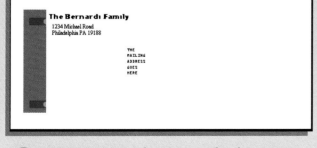

Designing an envelope is easy: There's not a great deal of room to play around with graphics because you have to leave room for the mailing address and the stamp. Print this publication and take it to a quick print business to have family envelopes.

For When You Care to Make Your Very Best

Having a party? Need to send a birthday card or another type of card to celebrate an occasion? Don't run to the gift shop or the drug store, run to your computer and fire up Publisher.

There's nothing more personal or more thoughtful than using your own words and your own design when you send a card. And sometimes there might be an occasion for which the stores don't sell cards. Your cousin's cat is having a birthday? Getting spayed? Send a card.

▶ **1** Making a card is simple when you have the PageWizard to help. Choose Card & Invitation and choose OK. Then choose the type of card you want to create and click Next.

6 All the pages print on the same piece of paper. Fold the paper properly and your card is ready to send.

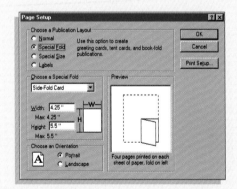

5 Cards have a special layout and they're printed to match it. Choose File, Page Setup to see the way the card is laid out (and get hints about how to fold it properly).

2 Depending upon your choices, you'll be asked to make several choices and answer questions. For most cards, Publisher offers to show you suggested text. If you find something you like you can use it. You can also change it after it's inserted in your card.

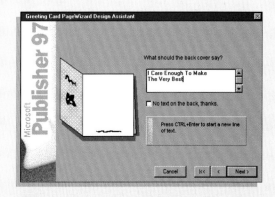

3 Continue to answer Publisher's requests for information, choosing Next to move to the next window. For some cards, such as invitations, you'll be asked to supply the date and time. Other cards have other specific text needs. You even get a chance to put a phrase on the back of the card.

4 Publisher takes your information, cogitates for a moment or two, then displays the front of your card. Click the page arrows on the Status bar to move through the four pages of the card (front, inside left, inside right, back). Feel free to add a picture frame, complete with clip art, to any blank space. You might even want to add a text box and create an additional message.

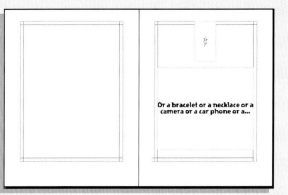

Things That Fold Funny, Fly Around, and Provide Fun

Not everything in Publisher's bag of tricks has a practical use. There are a few things you can create just to have some fun.

Origami, the ancient art of paper folding, has fascinated children and adults for thousands of years. A piece of paper gets folded, twisted, and bent, and suddenly becomes a beautiful ornament or a graceful bird. Your Publisher version comes complete with folding directions. The picture in the center of this section is, believe it or not, a crane. Well, it will be when it's folded.

And what's more fun than a paper airplane? The ones I made as a child soared beautifully for about two inches before plummeting to the ground. With the help of Publisher's PageWizard, I can print the fold lines so it's done right.

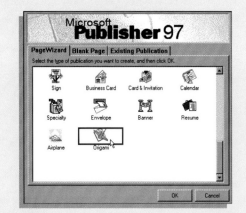

▶ 1 Like the other projects in this chapter, start with the PageWizard by choosing File, Create New Publication. Then click on Origami and choose OK.

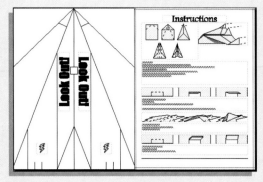

6 Your airplane is ready to soar. Print it, fold it, and fly it.

TIP SHEET

▶ **Print your projects on color paper to add flair.**

▶ **If you choose the radio as an airplane accessory, Publisher flashes a sarcastic comment.**

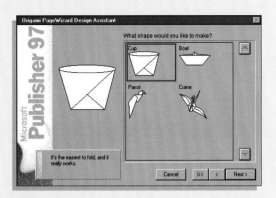

2 After an explanation of what origami is (choose Next when you finish reading it), choose a project. The cup holds water, the boat floats, the parrot is a little more difficult to fold, and the crane is positively daunting to create. Choose a cup, then choose Next.

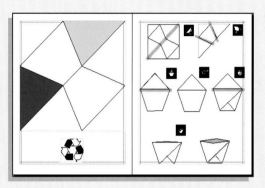

3 You can choose a color scheme if you wish (without a color printer it's just shades of gray), then Publisher displays the final design. Hard to believe that flat design is a cup in waiting. Move to the next page to see the directions. Then print your publication (the design prints first, then the directions page follows). Spend the next week trying to make a cup.

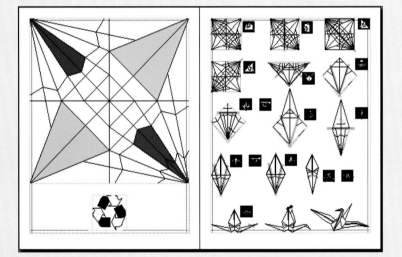

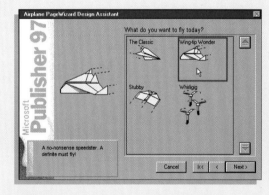

4 Start the PageWizard again and pick the airplane. Then decide what type of plane you want.

5 Pick your accessories. Then you can pick colors and a slogan that will appear on the side of the plane (if you fold it correctly), and a graphic. You can also decide if you want the folding instructions on a separate page, on the same page, or if you want to live on the edge and not print instructions at all.

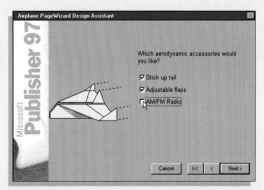

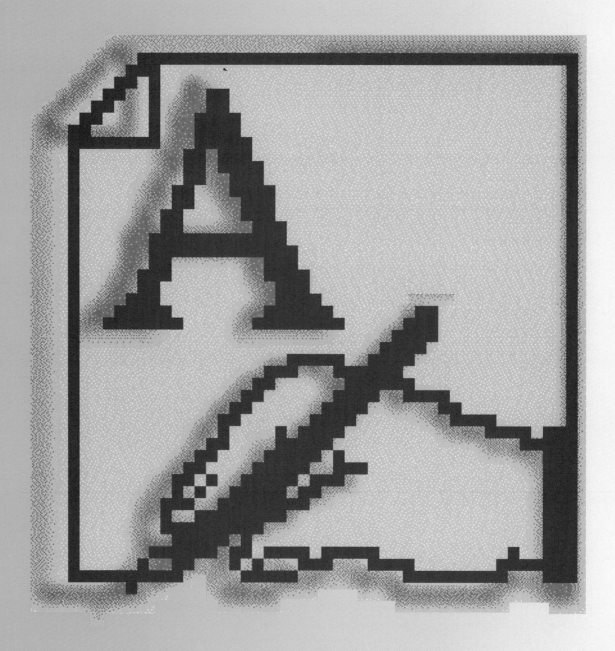

CHAPTER 22

Mail Merge

There are a number of business mailings that go to the same list over and over again: newsletters, promotional and marketing materials, catalogs, brochures, and other regularly scheduled publications. The same is true of your personal mail; you probably have a list of people who get cheerful cards from you every December.

You don't have to start all over again by compiling the list and addressing envelopes when a publication has to be distributed via snail mail (that's computer jargon for the regular postal service, which is much slower than e-mail). You can create lists, and then automate the process of sending a publication to the members of those lists.

In this chapter you'll learn how to create a mailing list, link a publication to it (or to members of the list who meet certain criteria), and even how to personalize the contents of the publication for each member of the list.

How to Create Lists

When you're using mail merge, you have to have a source file for the data (the names) and a target publication. In Publisher, the data source is called an address list.

In this section you'll learn how to create an address list.

▶ **1** Choose Mail Merge, Create Publisher Address List from the menu bar.

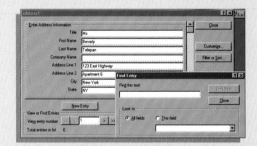

 You can choose New Entry to add more members to the list. Or you can view a specific entry (click the single arrow to move forward or back one entry, click the double arrow to move to the first or last entry). Choose Find Entry to search for one specific record.

TIP SHEET

▶ **You don't have to fill in every field for every record. However, the fields that are obviously necessary (name, address, city, state, and zip code) should be considered mandatory.**

▶ **When you use the Find Entry feature, the text you enter can be in any field in any record. If you want to narrow it down, enter the text then instruct Publisher to look in a specific field for that text.**

2 The New Address List dialog box opens with a blank new entry form. Each item in the dialog box is called a *field*, and you must fill in the appropriate information for each field. There are more fields than you see on this dialog box and you use the scroll bar to keep moving through them. As you complete each person's information (called a *record*), choose New Entry to bring up another blank record.

3 Choose Close when you have finished entering records. The Save As dialog box displays so you can save this address book. Enter a name for it, then choose Save. Publisher adds the file extension .MDB automatically.

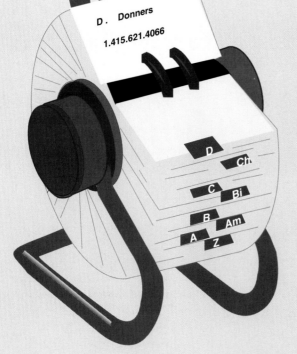

4 To return to this address list and work on it, choose Mail Merge, Edit Publisher Address List.

5 The Open Address List dialog box opens and displays all the address lists you've created. Double-click on the one you want to work with.

How to Merge Lists into Your Publication

Now that you have a data source, you can create a publication and link all or some of the records in an address list to it. This means you can address an envelope or a label to the specific people (records) that should receive the publication. And you can enter data from fields within the text of the publication, for example saying, "How are you <first name>?"

▶1 In your publication, create a text frame where you want to place information from the data source (or click the spot in an existing text frame).

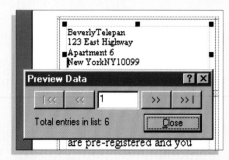

6 Choose Mail Merge, Merge. The information in the fields replaces the field names in your publication and there are as many pages as there are records. Publisher displays a dialog box so you can preview the results. Choose Close and print your publication by choosing File, Print Merge. A page will print for each record.

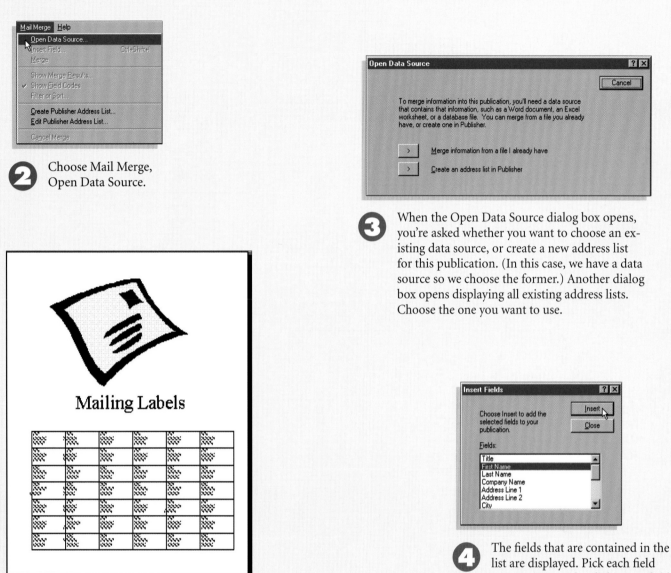

2 Choose Mail Merge, Open Data Source.

Mailing Labels

3 When the Open Data Source dialog box opens, you're asked whether you want to choose an existing data source, or create a new address list for this publication. (In this case, we have a data source so we choose the former.) Another dialog box opens displaying all existing address lists. Choose the one you want to use.

4 The fields that are contained in the list are displayed. Pick each field you want to use by clicking its field name, then clicking Insert. When you have added all the fields you need, choose Close.

5 The fields are placed in your publication. Use the Enter key to separate them into discrete lines. You can add punctuation, spaces or any text you wish.

How to Sort and Select from Mailing Lists

Sometimes you don't want to send a publication to everyone on the list. Perhaps you just need to notify people in a specific state about an event. Or maybe only the people who work at a specific corporation need to receive mail from you.

Perhaps you want to sort your mailing in a certain way, the common choice being zip code, because you can save money on large mailings if you presort by the zip codes.

Publisher lets you make several choices regarding the recipients of your mail merge.

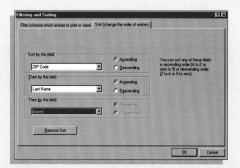

The seminar for Pennsylvania customers is being held on April 22, at 9AM. You are pre-registered and you may pick up your badge at the Information Desk.

1 Create your publication, inserting the fields in the appropriate place as described in the preceding section. Choose Mail Merge, Open Data Source and select the list you want to use.

6 To sort the records, use the Sort tab of the Filtering and Sorting dialog box. Select the fields you want to sort by, indicating whether you want them in ascending or descending order.

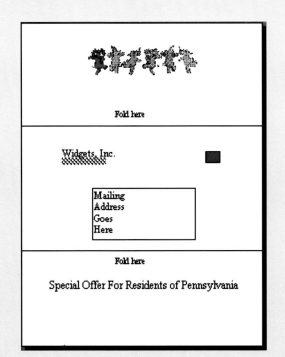

2 Choose Mail Merge, Filter or Sort from the menu bar. The Filtering and Sorting dialog box displays so you can begin defining the way you want to filter (select) records or sort (change the order in which the records are compiled).

3 To select specific records, click the arrow in the Field box and choose the field you want to use as a criteria.

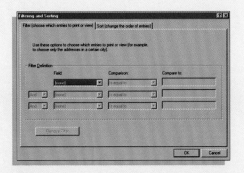

4 Select the Comparison you want to make in order to decide whether a record will be included. The choices are: Is equal to; Is not equal to; Is less than; Is greater than. Then enter the data you want to compare with the criteria. Click on OK.

5 Publisher selects only the records that match your selection criteria. To see the number of records and view the contents, choose Mail Merge, Show Merge Results.

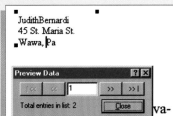

nia customers is being held

CHAPTER 23

Creating a Web Page with Publisher

Publications that are printed on the World Wide Web need some special handling. Luckily, if you plan to publish for the Web, Publisher has some built-in tools so that you don't have to worry about all the programming: It's all taken care of for you.

In fact, you can design and create a Web page in much the same way that you design a page for a regular publication. There are just a few easy-to-use Publisher tools to learn about that will take care of all the details needed to ensure your publication works on the Internet.

Publisher provides several methods for creating Web pages and you'll learn about them in this chapter. The features built into Publisher for creating and working with Web pages are plentiful and robust. This chapter presents a brief overview so that you can get an idea of how to use Publisher to create a Web page. After you're comfortable with the tools and features you learn about in this chapter, you'll be able to experiment with Publisher and learn the advanced concepts.

How to Start a Web Page with the PageWizard

If you want to try your first Web page with a lot of help from Publisher, you can use the PageWizard to get started. This gives you a chance to put your message into a preformatted design and go through the steps necessary to insert all the Web features your publication needs.

▶ **1** If you're just starting Publisher, the PageWizard appears automatically. If you're already working in Publisher, choose File, Create New Publication from the menu bar to bring up the PageWizard. Once the PageWizard is in your Publisher window, select Web Site and click OK.

TIP SHEET

▶ As you make decisions about background and color, it may be helpful to realize what happens when people access your Web site. First, they see the background. Then, the text appears. Finally, the graphics appear. Each element is drawn on the user's screen and it takes a bit of time for each element to complete. A plain (white) background isn't necessarily a negative feature if the text that appears against it is bold, attention getting, and colorful. If you have a lot of information you're presenting via text, you probably ought to think about an eye-catching background.

▶ The decisions you make as you step through the PageWizard windows aren't final. You can change every element on your Web page at any time.

6 The PageWizard presents a formatted Web page. Now you can begin to change the placeholder text and graphics to the specific information you want to place on the Web.

2 The PageWizard asks questions and wants you to make some decisions. First, select the type of Web site you're preparing your publication for, then click Next.

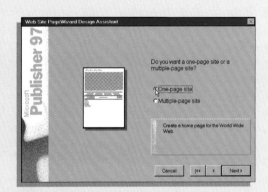

3 You have to decide if you want a one-page publication or a multiple-page publication. Until you've had some experience with designing and creating Web pages, it's probably best to do one page. Choose Next to move along.

4 Several more PageWizard questions appear so you can pick a style for your Web page (for example, classic or jazzy), and a background (plain, solid, or textured). Then this PageWizard window will appear and ask you to name your home page. This is the headline for your publication and, like all headlines, it should attract attention and be descriptive. Unfortunately, you're limited to 25 characters so you have to find a short, creative way to say, "Stop here and browse a minute." Choose Next after you've written your snappy headline.

5 There are a couple of additional PageWizard windows in which you decide whether you want your company's address or phone numbers on the page (if you do, you enter them in the PageWizard). Then the PageWizard creates a preformatted Web page that's ready for you to personalize. You're asked if you want step-by-step help as you finish your Web page, and if you respond Yes the Publisher Help files will open to give you advice as you work. If you respond No you can open the help files when you need them.

How to Customize Your Preformatted Web Page

Once the PageWizard has formatted the page, you can begin enter the specific text and graphics you need to make this Web page your own. You'll add text, select specific graphics, and make formatting changes. You can also change the background if you decide you didn't like the one you chose in the PageWizard.

As you enter the text and insert graphics, remember that if you're designing and creating a Web page for a business, your publication is a sales tool. Even if your Web page is established primarily to provide information, it should be worded and presented as if it were an advertisement. If this is a personal Web page or one for a community organization, you don't have to worry quite so much about slanting your content toward enhancing the bottom line.

▶ **1** Select one of the text frames (it's probably a good idea to start at the top and work your way down), and press F9 to zoom in on it. The placeholder text is selected (highlighted), so as soon as you type a character your replacement text fills the frame.

6 If you'd rather coordinate your own color schemes, picking individual backgrounds and text colors, click the Custom tab. Then go ahead and select a color and texture for your background, and choose colors for the text.

To replace the graphics the PageWizard chose with something more appropriate, right-click on the picture frame and choose Insert Clip Art.

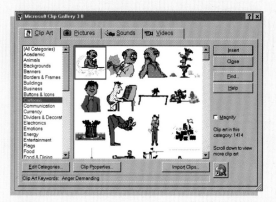

When the ClipArt Gallery opens, choose a category and a graphic that matches the message you're trying to convey on your Web page. You might want to look in the categories available in the Pictures tab.

To change the background motif of your Web page, right-click on any part of the page that doesn't have a frame. When the menu appears, choose Background and Text Colors.

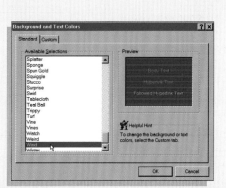

When the Background and Text Colors dialog box opens, the Standard tab is in the forefront. You can scroll through the list of Available Selections to choose a design scheme. These schemes are color-coordinated to work effectively. Most of the time the title text colors work quite well against the background.

How to Enter Hyperlinks and Test and Publish Your Web Page

A hyperlink is a pointer to another page. In fact, it's more than a pointer, it's an express train you can hop on to get to that page. When you click a hyperlink, you are immediately taken to the linked page on the Web. (While technically you can have a hyperlink to another section of the same page, this feature is generally used to move to another page.) Incidentally, the linked page doesn't have to be one of your own Web pages, and there are plenty of Web sites that provide hyperlinks to other Web sites. Text and graphics are both candidates for hyperlink pointers.

TIP SHEET

▶ The choices in the Hyperlink dialog box include: a document already on the Internet, which means you have to enter the Web site address where that document resides; another page in your Web site, which requires an entry specifying the page; an Internet e-mail address, which means you must enter that address; and a file on your hard disk, which requires a path to that file (the file is downloaded from your Web site to the user's hard drive).

▶ When you're previewing your page in a browser, if you click on a hyperlink that is not connected to your own Web page, a real session will start in order to test the link. Your dial-up software will launch and you'll have to log on to the Internet to complete the test.

▶ For the Internet e-mail address option, you can enter your own e-mail address so that clicking on the hyperlink sends you a message.

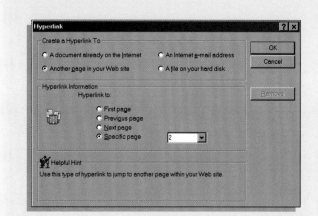

❶ To create a text hyperlink, select (highlight) the text that you want to use. To create a graphic hyperlink, click the picture frame to select it. Then (for either selection) choose Insert, Hyperlink (or press Ctrl+K). The Hyperlink dialog box appears. There are four choices for hyperlinks, and the Hyperlink Information box in the middle of the dialog box changes depending upon the type of hyperlink you choose. See the Tip Sheet on this page for more details about hyperlink types. For a text hyperlink, the selected text changes color and is underlined. When it's on your Web page, clicking on it will move the user to the linked page you establish. For a graphic hyperlink, you won't see any changes in the graphic.

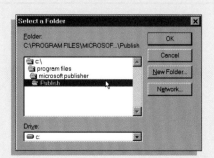

❻ If you want to use this publication internally (like a local intranet), publish it to a folder on your hard drive. Make sure other users on the network can access that folder (ask your network administrator about creating shared folders).

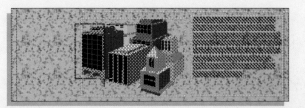

2 You can also create a hyperlink to a specific part of a graphic frame instead of the entire frame. This is called a hot spot and it's useful for linking different parts of a graphic to different pages. To perform this feat, first click the Picture Hot Spot tool on the Publisher toolbar. (When you are creating a Web page, the Picture Hot Spot tool is added to the Publisher toolbar.)

3 Put your pointer on upper-left corner of the hot spot you want to create. Click and hold the left mouse button while you drag a box around the area that will become the hot spot. When you release the mouse button, the Hyperlink dialog box opens and you can fill it out as described in step 1.

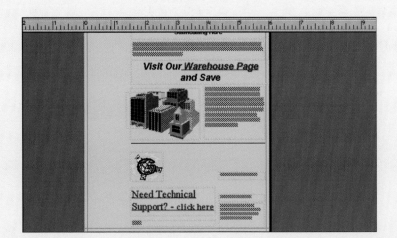

4 You can't tell much about the way the hyperlink will look on the Web while you're working in Publisher and you cannot, of course, tell whether the link works. You have to check your work by running a mock Web session. (This assumes you have installed Web browser software.) Choose File, Preview Web Site. Your browser launches and places your Web publication in its window (the modem is not accessed and you are not really connected to the Internet; it just seems as if you are).

5 Once everything is right, you can publish your Web page on your Web site. You must have the Web Publishing Wizard (which doesn't come with the Publisher software). If you don't have the Wizard, Publisher will open your browser and your dial-up software, go to the correct Microsoft page, and download it for you. Then use the Wizard to publish your page by answering the questions and following the instructions. It's all quite simple.

INDEX